"When Horses Whisper you can listen! Read Rosalyn Berne."

—Rita Mae Brown, MFH, author of the *Mrs. Murphy* mystery series, and the *Sneaky Pie Brown* mystery series

"I started my practice as a veterinarian six years ago, and did not have any particular interest in horses. Working in a small rural town in Costa Rica, I have to deal with all animals that need my service, including cows, dogs, cats, goats, sheep, and of course, horses. I began to feel something special when I had a horse as a patient, a feeling of peace that I do not have with any other animal. And attracted by that feeling, I worked more and more frequently with horses. At that point, I did not realize what was going on. With Rosa's book, I began to realize that I was not the only one who was giving a service. Horses also give a service to me. Her book helped me to understand how the horse-human relationship works. Besides, I learned many lessons about how we should treat horses as living beings that deserve respect. And if we could extrapolate these lessons to our daily life, we will grow as human beings in peace and harmony with every being that surrounds us."

—Daniel Zeledon-Donzo, D.V.M.

WHEN
THE
HORSES
WHISPER

The Wisdom of Wise
and Sentient Beings

ROSALYN W. BERNE

RAINBOW RIDGE
BOOKS

Cover and Interior design by Frame25 Productions
Cover photograph © mariait c/o Shutterstock.com

Published by:
Rainbow Ridge Books, LLC
140 Rainbow Ridge Road
Faber. Virginia 22938
434-361-1723

If you are unable to order this book from your local
bookseller, you may order directly from the distributor.

Square One Publishers, Inc.
115 Herricks Road
Garden City Park, NY 11040
Phone: (516) 535-2010
Fax: (516) 535-2014
Toll-free: 877-900-BOOK

Visit the author at:
www.whenthehorseswhisper.com

Library of Congress Cataloging-in-Publication Data applied for.

ISBN 978-1-937907-16-7

10 9 8 7 6 5 4 3 2 1

Printed on acid-free paper in the United States

DEDICATION

To the memory of Aladdin, my childhood equine friend, and to all the horses of the world who live and work in the service and companionship of human beings.

ACKNOWLEDGMENTS

Thanks go to Steve and Debbie Legg of Leaves and Lizards-Arenal Volcano Cabin Retreat in Costa Rica for providing me direct access to their horses, and for their kindness and generosity in support of my communicating with them. Without Debbie, my muse, this book would probably never have been written. Mis amigos Enrique, Ronald, Chito, Erick, Juan José, Ocsar and Cendri; I am astounded by your refined horsemanship. Thank you for trusting me and for listening when I hear. And to my horse friends: Titán, Conan, J.R, Beauty, Mr. Big, Juano, Gitana, Amarillo, Suzy, Pica, Dorado, Cortessa, Penina, Caretto, Diana, Ringo; for you there are no words. Of course not, because it's not with words that we communicate. So in our wordless way, I thank you. Because of you, I have learned to feel and sense more deeply, and become a person I never knew I could be.

In the U.S.A., I thank Priscilla Friedberg and her horses, especially Blue Star, as they have been gracious and helpful in this project; Bill Prindle, my beloved, who sees me for who I am and brings that out in my writing; Mariah Dean who helped me to surrender to what truly needed to be written, and Kathleen Manuel, my editor, who guided me to craft just the right words in just the right way to express what I wish to say— my heartfelt thanks. Bob Friedman, my publisher, not only believes that I hear the horses, but has encouraged me to teach others how, and made it possible for me to share it in this book. Through the lenses and keen eyes of photographer Kaya Berne, the horses' personalities and essence are captured beautifully in the images included. My deepest appreciation to you all.

A portion of the proceeds from the sale of *When the Horses Whisper* will be donated to equine-assisted therapy programs.

TABLE OF CONTENTS

FOREWORD

Rosalyn (Rosa) Berne brings the whispered voice of the horses themselves to remind us to wake up and live consciously in our interconnectedness, to open our hearts and our ears, to allow ourselves to heal the trauma no human or horse escapes in these times.

No new age eccentric adolescent, Rosa is a mature, wise, and compassionate woman, a professor and a mother, grounded and sensible.

What she hears from the horses rings true. Those of us who love and respect the horses as the wise sentient beings they are, get lots of non-verbal wisdom from them. Rosa receives a deeper level of information, through a capacity she calls clairaudience, about their life histories, their sufferings and their wishes and needs. It was a privilege to travel with her on a horse trek and witness firsthand how she helps us understand the horses' perspective.

If horses spoke out loud these are the heart opening and heart breaking messages I would expect to hear. "Be kind, be clear, be respectful, be loving, and be faithful and consistent."

As a practicing psychiatrist and equine facilitated psychotherapist, I find Dr. Berne's stories from the horses to be useful, fun, and powerfully instructive.

This book is a gift to all of us who love horses and are dedicated to their work of helping us to open and heal our human hearts.

Nancy Coyne, M.D., Psychiatrist

I

BENEDICTION

Horses have the capacity to help us heal the human heart. Let us stand in their presence with openness and faith.

These beings left the realm of existence that is the "*soul-of-horse*" and chose to labor in the service of humans. They are not angels, but are rather our companions on a journey that none of us controls but that, if we trust it, can guide us to places we have always longed to be.

This journey is not generic or abstract; it is intensely personal. It calls us to re-member, to put back together, our whole selves in the wholeness of creation. It requires us to face the parts of us that we split off, denied, and placed in shadow because they were too painful. Horses can help us find these lost parts, and call forth our courage to reclaim them.

Horses are here on the earth because we need them. This has been true for thousands of years, although the ways in which we need them have evolved. They have consented to enter into loving service to us, out of their instinctual concern for our wellbeing, and for our mutual purposes of spiritual growth. What other animals have literally carried us on their backs for purposes of war, recreation, farming, hunting, showmanship, and competitive sport? What other beings have accompanied us on long and arduous journeys across difficult terrain that would have been impossible for us without their help, and more recently have provided us with physical therapy and emotional support as well?

How incredible that the Divine reaches us through communication with the non-human world, for deeper consubstantiality.

II

COMPANIONS ON OUR JOURNEY

This book expresses in human language what horses have to say when given the chance to speak. It is a story about the bond between horse and human, and the communication made possible when the bond is based on love. It recounts the equine healing work that helped in reclaiming my authentic self, a testimony to the power of horses in transforming our losses into a deeper human wholeness. For me, these included miscarriage followed by the loss of a newborn daughter, the mental illness of an adult son, the end of a thirty-year marriage, and a traumatic childhood sexual encounter. Conversations with fifteen horses, most of who live and work in Costa Rica, are featured along with their photographs, capturing them as individual beings in service to humans on a shared evolutionary journey.

I am not a "horse person." I have never owned a horse. I don't ride regularly, nor am I skilled in handling horses. But I have been touched by the *soul-of-horse*, and have been humbly honored to receive a gift, a "*don de Dios*" as a Costa Rican horseman called it, which has enabled me to sense and bring to human expression the thoughts of these wondrous creatures. I share the treasure I have received in communicating with these beings so that other people may better understand their inner world, and the ways it can help us understand our own. And for those who ride or own horses, I tell this story as another way for you to learn to trust what you hear when your horse needs to speak.

The horses I have spoken with over the last two and a half years have given me tremendous support in my own journey of personal transformation. They entered my reality and helped me change how I see my life. The emotional dynamics of my early childhood had left me with a heavy sense of responsibility for others—the students I teach, my family, the homeless people I pass on the street. I also felt responsible to be strong and intelligent, healthy, and accomplished, a beacon of success for my extended family and community. This ingrained sense of responsibility came with a price: it sat like a lid on top of deeper feelings of sorrow and grief, served to preserve the illusion of being in control, and also tamped down the terror of losing that precious control. It took encounters with remarkable horses to make me feel and accept, deep in my core, just how powerless I am over many elements of my life. Without these horses, I might not have gone to that depth, might not have touched that fear or felt that grief, or come to the profound realizations I received. I discovered that life need not feel so burdensome, that pain and uncertainty can be carried more lightly, that there are many other beings here to help, if we allow them into our hearts.

Horses have a profound capacity to communicate directly and in detail with humans, although of course they don't use spoken human language. But their pre-linguistic and sometimes visual mode of expression can be understood in human-language terms if one is open to the experience. The horses featured here are highly perceptive, sensitive, and aware. They are offering their hearts to connect deeply with their human companions. And they have a lot to say!

People often ask me, "How and when did you learn to communicate with horses?" The short answer is that it happened a few years ago, while riding a horse in Costa Rica. But when I reach back in memory I find that my ability to sense the thoughts and feelings of horses started many years ago, when I was a child living in Philadelphia.

In the city, life was loud. We lived on a main artery, Wayne Avenue, in the Germantown neighborhood. Wayne was busy day and night with buses, cars, electric trolleys that rattled on old steel rails, racing police vehicles, and ambulances with blaring sirens. Freight and passenger trains rumbled along the Reading Line. Frequent family gatherings added the buzz of gossiping aunts, gathered in our kitchen with my grandmother. The women cooked while uncles sank into upholstered chairs in the living room, beer cans in hand and cigarettes hanging from their lips, yelling at the Phillies or the Eagles on the black and white screen, or arguing over politics or current affairs.

Outdoors, children played stickball on the tarred streets. Hand-made box carts and roller-skates screeched beneath the shouting voices. Girls played double-dutch with blurring ropes, rhythmically brushing the cement squares of the sidewalk. The cacophony of laughing, shouting, and cursing in that neighborhood swirled around our house, sometimes gleeful, more often discordant, while inside, John Coltrane,

Thelonius Monk, Wolfgang Mozart, and Count Basie sustained a sweeter music on the high fidelity phonograph.

When I joined Girl Scout Junior troop # 139 at age 9, I discovered a new, quieter, and even richer side of the city. Led by a married couple with a passion for the outdoors, one Saturday we headed out of our church meeting place for a full day's hike in Fairmount Park. I thought I'd gone to heaven: I saw majestic trees that didn't just form the familiar man-made lines along city streets, but instead grew in a new and wilder order in a thick forest. Milky quartz and mica-tinged granite shimmered under flowing creeks. Huge rock outcrop-pings protruded from the hills as concrete bridges soared high above. Open fields grew wild flowers. I began to feel the quiet, as the city's hubbub grew distant.

And there were horses: I smelled them and saw their droppings along the trail. Toward the end of the day, we finally reached the stables. The sound of whinnying emanated from the dimly lit stalls where dark manes and heads appeared as massive shadows. Something stirred in me: *Who are these creatures?* I wondered. The fullest answer wouldn't come for nearly 45 years, though I had my first inkling two summers later with an Arabian horse named Aladdin.

Aladdin was one of the horses at Echo Farm Camp. Located northeast of Philadelphia in Bucks County, Echo Farm had the classic summer camp elements: "bunks" and "bug juice" and the like. I attended a two-week session the summer I turned eleven.

Camp's amenities brought great relief to us city kids: a swimming pond, walking trails, playing fields, yoga classes, campfires with "s'mores," guitars and singing, and arts and crafts. But my favorite was horseback riding. We were taught how to pass behind a horse to avoid being kicked, how to put on a saddle and bridle, and how to secure the black velvet riding helmets to our heads. Mounting and dismounting, mucking the stalls, and brushing and feeding the horses were part of our daily routine. We did most of our riding in an enclosed ring, English-style, so I was delighted on the days when we'd go out onto the fields and trails. It felt good to find out that under my direction a horse would go this way or that, and would stop, trot, and jump with me on its back.

Aladdin was a gray and white gelding. Riding him, I learned I could surrender to his gait, and enter a state of centered trust I hadn't known was possible. Reaching my hand through the fence rails to stroke his coarse mane, I was comforted by Aladdin's presence, at some deep level I had not sensed before. It was so relaxing for me to touch him, and to see his big round eyes, black and deep, opening wide at my presence. I felt as if he cared about me. When my hand stroked his cheeks, my lips touched his forehead, or my chest and shoulders pressed against his side, a sense of profound ease came over me. With Aladdin, I feared nothing.

There was plenty for a young girl to be afraid of back then: gangs that might erupt into violence, strange men attempting to fondle, and mean girls who threatened to beat me up for being different. I was afraid to walk those three long blocks down Wayne Avenue to Chelten to my Scout meetings, or to my elementary school on Greene Street. I was afraid I might pass the wrong place or person at the wrong time, and find myself in harm's way. I felt the fearsome presence of gangs like "Haines Street" and "Brickyard," who were rumored to roam near our home. I dreaded the empty parks where shadowy figures lurked behind bushes and inebriated men slumped on benches. I knew about the rough hands of grown men, powerless over everything else in their lives, who thrust themselves onto naive young girls like me.

Something sinister had happened to me, violated my body as a very young girl. I buried it farther and farther down in my subconscious but the symptoms continued to surface: recurring nightmares, nightly bedwetting, playing alone, making fires in secret, stealing and lying, and the sensation that I was not actually inhabiting my own body. The confusion over what was pleasurable and what was not, what was forbidden and what was appropriate, and the inability to utter the words, "No, don't do that," when my body was being invaded, all were signs that something terrible had been done to me, something my conscious mind had split off and refused to remember. The world was scary, I knew that much. And as I increasingly lost hold of myself I projected that terror onto the world around me.

But I found a safe place with Aladdin, whose great strength and tremendous heart gave me a feeling of being protected.

"If only I could keep him and take him back home," I thought. "Then everything would be okay."

Though happy to see my parents when they came for me at the end of summer camp, I begged them to let me stay longer. But it was not to be: they loaded my bags into the car and I said goodbye to my counselors and bunkmates. The last thing I did was to find Aladdin, grazing out in the pasture. He turned toward me as I waved my arms to get his attention.

"Aladdin!" I cried. "I've come to say goodbye." We stood together alone for several minutes while I stroked him. Choking back tears, I sensed him tell me:

Don't worry. I'll always be with you.

I mourned for months. I never forgot Aladdin. I spoke of him so often that next school year that a teacher gifted me with her childhood collection of ceramic horses. I placed them on my windowsill, where the sun made them shine. Reclining on my bed, I would stare at them, my imagination placing me bareback on those objects of beauty as we trotted off to magical, faraway places.

One Saturday that autumn, I walked back to the Fairmount Park stables. I found a woman working with the horses and asked her if I could volunteer in exchange for riding privileges. She agreed, and I went back the following Saturday but was told there were no available horses to ride. Willing to work, thinking I might build up credit for next time, she handed me a shovel and showed me where to find a barrel. For the next hour I went from one dark stall to the next, shoveling out the manure. Nearly finished, I heard the sound of a hoof pounding the ground from the last stall. I put down the shovel, peering between the boards: a chestnut Quarter Horse looked back at me. He was bigger than any horse I had ever seen, but something compelled me to unlatch the gate, and before I knew it I was in the stall with him.

"Hello there, big boy," I said, stroking his side and neck. He told me of his sadness, how unseen and unheard he felt. Because I often felt the same, I sympathized with him. Though I felt powerless to help him, I just stood by his side. I went back the following Saturday, and was again disappointed in being told that it wasn't a convenient day for me to ride. I stayed and worked, hoping at least to see my new friend. But he wasn't there—he must have been out on the trail.

On the third Saturday my mother forbade me from going, pointing out insistently that I was being taken advantage of. I knew she was right, and did not return, but I regret that I never got to tell the beautiful chestnut horse goodbye.

III

HEARING WHEN THEY SPEAK

In the four and a half decades since being with Aladdin, my understanding of horses has deepened along with my life experience and inner growth. As I've gained clarity and strength in myself and my ways of experiencing the world, my willingness to be more public in communicating what I know has also become stronger.

Today I experience horses as expressions of the loving, healing *soul-of-horse*, but when I was a child I kept my soul connections with horses secret, scrawled across the lines of my diary and locked away with a tiny key. Today I am moved to share my experiences, along with the thoughts, concerns, and desires of the horses I meet. I am moved to do this because I have a deep sense that horses feel a more urgent need for humans to hear them, and that humans have a more urgent need for the understanding and the healing that horses offer us. I believe this enhanced communication is as much about people as it is about horses, and that what these magnificent animals have to tell us bears deep significance for our awakening as human beings. Perhaps *soul-of-horse* has graciously gifted me with this ability to facilitate the deeper and richer journey that our two species can explore together.

People often ask how it is that I can communicate with horses, how it works, and what I do. As for what makes it possible, that remains a mystery. I experience it as an emergence of something from within me, but not *of* me, although I don't know myself exactly how it works and I continue to seek to understand the process. Perhaps that's a question for the cognitive scientists. Then again, is there any point in trying to dissect the capacity of one species to connect with another? On Earth, all species of life, all organisms, are interconnected and evolving together.

That being said, I will try to put into words the process I go through when I communicate with a horse.

As a child, I believed all things were possible. I knew then, as we all do at birth, that the Life Force within us also connects us. We experience ourselves as one with mother, and also with the life around us. But as our sense of self takes hold, we begin to become separate individuals, falling from the grace state of awareness of our connection with God into the mental perception of separation. But the separation is only in our minds. In fact, the Source of our being continues to maintain its connection to us, and it flows among all of life as an energy connecting all living creatures. This is how it is possible for humans and horses to communicate with each other.

As we grow further into our sense of separation and individuality, language arises from imitating those around us, and we begin to sense and believe, mistakenly, that is it the language itself which is being communicated. But the words are merely the medium. What is being communicated is actually the energetic flow of divine substance moving between us, as us.

When I hear horses, I move in that flow of connection with them, and then I translate what they express into my own language. So it doesn't matter whether a horse lives in Costa Rica and has heard only Spanish all his life, or in the United States where people have spoken to him exclusively in English. The horse can understand me and I him because we communicate with each other in a pre-linguistic state of interconnectedness. We listen to each other inside of that flow which unifies our souls.

God speaks to humans in the same way. The still, small voice spoken of in the Christian Bible is "still" and "small" because it is silent. We translate what we hear in prayer into our own language, and that translation becomes our scriptures, sermons, hymns, chants, and poems.

When I say that I "hear" horses, I'm not referring to an auditory process involving the ear, but rather to an inner hearing that arises from a quiet state of being. To hear horses whisper is much like hearing an answer to a prayer, and in both cases we have to trust and believe what we hear with our mind's ear. God's language is silent, and so is the language of horses. Humans have the same ability to communicate without spoken words, but in many of us it has become atrophied through lack of use. We can relearn that way of relating, though, if we can learn to let go (if just for a little while) of our sense of separateness. When we move into a state of deep connection to the unity of life, language falls away.

Many of us claim to hear God speak to us, but God hasn't the embodiment needed to form words and to utter them. So how is it we "hear" God?

To hear what God tells us, we use our inward ears, which carry God's message to our heart. We hear God without a single word spoken when we shift to an awareness of our connection with God, because God moves and has his being within us, as us. Since God also moves between us as the life force of all being, all creatures of this earth are connected to one another through God. It is this connection that makes it possible to hear horses whisper.

And so I begin each session with the horses by cultivating a state of awareness in which my mind is quiet and open to the soul-of-horse. This is the state I refer to as release, where I put aside language and reliance on the physical apparatus of the hearing sense in order to shift into the neutrality needed to believe and trust in a process that does not involve words, but instead is based on the connection of the mind and heart. God can be heard speaking to us only when we've centered ourselves in a deep state of silent being. The process works the same with horses, and if horse and human open themselves one to the other in the essence of an energetic state of unity, real communication becomes possible.

Above all, I need to be comfortable and feel safe around the horse. The surroundings, the horse's behavior, and my own emotional state all play a role in how comfortable I feel, but I always have to have a certain amount of control. The calmer and more self-assured I am, the more the horse is able to trust me.

As I approach the horse, I explain to him or her who I am and why I'm there. I tell them that if they want to talk, I will be able to understand what they say. Meanwhile, the horse senses my aura and state of being, and reads my true intentions. In fact, the horse starts to get a sense of me the moment I walk into the stable or barn. Horses are extremely perceptive.

Moving closer and closer, I whisper directly into his or her ear. The most important determinant of a successful communication is the horse's understanding that I mean him or her no harm, and that my purpose is authentic. I place my hand gently on the horse's body. This touch, I have discovered, is not essential to the communication, but can help me to sense the spirit of the horse. In fact, there have been occasions when I have been able to communicate with a horse at a distance, from the other side of a barn or even from thousands of miles away.

Sometimes the horse moves away, indicating that they have no interest or perhaps no desire or need to communicate with me. Or the horse may step away but then return to my side, ready to be heard. Often horses indicate their desire to speak by staring intently at me from afar. My next step depends upon the horse's response, its personality, and the circumstances. The presence of the horse's owner can either help or not, depending on their relationship.

Throughout my conversation with the horse, I remind him or her often that I want to listen, and that I will share what he or she tells me with the owner. Some horses respond immediately, while others take some time to open up to me. Usually the horse will stand very still as we communicate. Sometimes, the horse will make licking and chewing motions and lower its head. This is a sign that the horse is submitting to me, or affirming the accuracy of my interpretations, or both. There are occasions when a horse may seem to be ignoring me, such as when he lowers his head to eat hay while I am speaking. Even so, a flow of communication between us may still be taking place.

To understand what the horses are saying, I have to shift my state of mind from a place that is linguistically oriented, visually dominated and intellectually judging, to a state where I am intuitively present, open and observing. Allowing my consciousness to spread out, I leave the confines of the cerebral cortex and extend my awareness down into my solar plexus. (This may not be a scientific way of describing it, but it is how one horse explained what I needed to do to extend our communication.) All of my senses then become exquisitely keen. Colors and sounds become intensely vibrant, and certain scents are so strong that they leave an impression on my tongue. But what I call 'releasing' is the most heightened of my senses.

To release, I must let go and trust, dropping entirely into the fullness of the present moment to allow my perceptions to shift beyond the five senses, and it is absolutely essential that I do this in order to understand the information coming from the horse. As with driving a standard transmission car, it's a matter of shifting into neutral, with the gears one through five representing each of the five senses. I must 'shift into neutral' and let go of the control I normally have over my senses, a control that makes living in the day to day world possible but at the same time limits my capacity to perceive on the level of the soul-of-horse. This shift into neutral makes it possible to 'hear,' to sense with my entire being, and allows my full mind, including my bodily senses, to inform what I perceive. The communication may be only momentary, or it may last fifteen minutes or more. The process, however, does not rely entirely on my ability to release. I can only hear the horse when the horse is willing to engage, and to communicate we must both be in a mutuality of connecting.

When I was a young girl, I could hear and understand what horses were communicating. Only recently has that ability re-emerged, in the middle of a very difficult year. With the disintegration of a 30-year marriage and subsequent breakup of my beloved family, I was emotionally drained. I was working in a senior level position for a not-for-profit organization that was struggling to survive. Fifty-hour workweeks and no vacation for well over a year had left me entirely spent. Under the loss of what was most important to me (family life and home), my career motivation was rapidly waning. Living alone for the first time in my life, the white walls of my new condominium home seemed to be closing in on me. I dreamed of taking refuge in a remote, distant place where I could unwind, grieve and reflect.

It had been a long while since I'd had the time to work on a novel I was writing, and I yearned to get back to that project. Most important, I needed to rest and restore myself. So I headed for a place I was familiar with, where the beauty and richness of nature would nourish and restore my spirit: the northern mountains of Costa Rica in sight of the Arenal volcano. I'd traveled there three times before, though never by myself, and with each visit I felt myself increasingly drawn to the land.

On one of those previous trips, I was with my family hiking not far from Rincón de la Vieja Volcano National Park. We stopped in amazement at the sight of a petroglyph carved into the rock face just above the trail. The sight of it took my breath away, and I was overcome with the feeling that the ancient imagery was familiar, that I actually understood what it meant. I cannot explain how or why.

I responded even more emotionally to the volcano Arenal. We'd arrived just before nightfall to the town of La Fortuna. Gleefully, we watched the glowing red lava tumbling down the side of the cone-shaped mountain. Early the next morning, we took a twenty-minute guided walk through a forest along an ascending dirt road. When we reached the wide clearing at the end, the volcano loomed above us. It was magnificent, in full view from base to cone, and no more than a few football fields away. I gazed in silent awe, contemplating the significance of the geologic marvel. And then I heard it: the gases exchanging rhythmically, like exhalations and inhalations, moving into and out of the volcano, a deep rumbling that made me realize that the mountain was breathing. I dropped to my knees in tears, recognizing that the earth is an animate organism, and in fact is really, truly, *alive*.

Years later, Arenal's magnetic force tugged on me again. I felt it when I was beyond exhausted, at a loss for how to reassemble what had been my wonderful life. My husband and I were divorcing and I was making the final move out. Our son was in his fifth year of rough and rapid cycles of manic psychotic episodes and showed little sign of improvement. Our daughter, experiencing her own reasons for distress, withdrew from university and returned to her father's house, the only home she knew. Gone was my belief in the existence of God, and my sense of connection to the Divine.

I felt the pull of Arenal's energy. It was an enticement to go back, to settle into its silent, majestic presence and to breathe in its potency and the richness of the surrounding land. It was a call to be healed and restored. I hadn't realized at the time that it was also an invitation to begin a process of deep personal, transformation.

IV

EQUINE ENCOUNTERS: TITÁN SPEAKS

Gathered just outside the exit doors of the Juan Santamaría International Airport is a crowd of taxi and hotel shuttle drivers. A man with a broad smile holds a sign with my name in bold, black type. "Mi nombre es Enrique," he says, honoring my attempt to speak and understand his language. A three-hour car ride takes us through the busy little city of San Ramon, over the fog-covered mountains beyond it, along winding roads, through wide valleys, and across rushing rivers to the tiny town of Monterrey. From there we take an unpaved, rutted, stone-strewn road about two miles up a steep hill. "You are not lost," one sign reads as we turn the first bend. "You are almost there," reads another as we take the last hill, past "Tico"-style concrete homes and the neighborhood Super Kiki store, finally arriving at our destination.

An Internet search had led me to book accommodations at the cabin retreat, but on arriving I was convinced it was actually providence. This was an ideal place for self-renewal, a remote spot with cabins in the rain forest within full view of Volcán Arenal, where the owners provide a full breakfast and dinner. An ex-patriot couple from the United States created the small eco-resort, which is also a working farm with chickens, pigs, cows, and horses. I checked in and was taken to a tree house-like cabin called Volcano, which is a ten-minute walk through lush tropical plantings on a steep, rutted driveway of stone and dirt.

On the first full day of my retreat, I focus intently from dawn until dinner on edits to the manuscript. I relish the opportunity to reconnect with the novel's characters, and to immerse myself in the fictional world I'd created. Indeed, it feels wonderful to write again, and I venture out only for meals. I walk the hilly dirt road at 7:00 a.m. for breakfast and at 7:00 p.m. for dinner, back and forth from my cabin to the open-air dining hall. Throughout the day, I take brief respites from the writing by relaxing in the hammock on the cabin's covered deck.

Hanging there in the splendor of nature, I observe the abundance of life all around. Blue-tinted hummingbirds stop to draw nectar from the flowering bushes below the cabin. Laughing falcons, perched high on tree limbs, rev themselves into hysteria. Colorful toucans with wide, extended beaks hop across branches obscured by broad green leaves, and in the distance, howler monkeys call with such deep and powerful voices that they give the impression of being much larger mammals. Birds of prey swoop and dive in their hunt for snakes while the sweet, moist air and huge-leafed flora lulls me into a state of relaxation. But it is the sight of Arenal in the distance that inspires the creative flow within me.

It rains often during my stay, torrential bursts pounding the cabin's metal roof from late afternoon into the early evening. The rain comes hard and fast, bringing a chill to the mountain air. The sound of the downpour is unbearably loud, making concentration on writing nearly impossible. I huddle under a blanket, perch upright on my bed, and stare at the cabin's huge picture window, my view obscured by a falling sheet of water. A thick mass of dark gray clouds dominates the sky, overcoming the glow of the setting sun, and night-fall follows close behind. Suddenly the downpour ends and a clear night sky emerges, the deep black of it strewn with bright, sparkling white stars. The sound of chirping crickets and frogs begins to rise.

On my second day at the mountain retreat I take a detour after breakfast, heading up to the stable rather than back down to my cabin home. I feel myself drawn inside, where eleven horses stand in stalls. It seems quiet when I first walk into the structure, perhaps because the place is new to me and so vision naturally dominates my other senses. But soon I become aware of the soft sounds of horses' movements: lips smacking and chewing, tails swishing, hoofs thumping, urine flowing, and the slow *clop clop clop* across the hard-packed surface of the dirt floor.

On the third day, I venture back to the stable after break-fast. Stable hands are washing down the horses in preparation for a trail ride, since they are dirty from spending the night out in the field. This is a quick visit, and I return right away to my cabin for another full day of writing.

On the fourth day, as has become my routine, I head out after breakfast to the stable, but the horses have been moved to the barn. It is Saturday, and they are there for *Vínculo con Caballo*, a therapeutic program created by Debbie, the co-owner of the lodge. *Vínculo* is Spanish for a deep, unexplainable connection between two souls, so the name of the program translates to "the horses bond." Debbie is a former pediatric nurse, and provides this service free of charge for disabled youth in the local community. These children, weak and compromised from their illnesses, perceive themselves as strong and capable while on horseback. I see the pride in the faces of the parents who stand nearby as their sons and daughters play games on horseback, and I observe the excited expressions on the children's faces. Most pronounced and heartening to me, however, is the depth of commitment and focus of the horses participating in the event.

I sign up for a trail ride the next day along with six other guests. We meet in the stable where we are fitted with helmets. Then we are given release forms to sign. Back at the barn the horses are saddled and waiting, and Debbie gives us a safety talk about riding. These are herd animals, she explains, which in the animal kingdom means they are prey. To them, humans are predators, unless we act as if we are part of their herd. Somewhat tongue-in-cheek, but mostly seriously, Debbie tells us that the horses will select the rider they want.

I am drawn to the horse named Titán.

"He always picks the person who will allow him to eat," she warns as I walk toward him. She is certainly right about that. From the moment I climb on his back until we return a few hours later, Titán grabs every clump of leaves he can get his mouth around. My commands to stop seem to carry no weight. Sure, he walks the trail with the other horses, but when he is finished chewing, Titán strays to the nearest greenery and grabs yet another mouthful. I am his sucker. Still, he is a joy to ride, despite the constant snacking.

The trail leads first to the summit of a hill where we have a dramatic and unobstructed view of the volcano. It is a clear afternoon and the volcano is fully visible, from broad base to narrow cone. Dormant now, it hasn't erupted in nearly a year, nor made any thunderous, rumbling sounds. All that is left of its activity is a thin trail of smoke floating from its open top. Nevertheless, it feels powerful and alive to me.

After taking a round of touristy "Look where I am!" photos, we continue our trek down to the river. Rio Arenal is swift, its clear water running over a sandy riverbed. When we arrive at the river's edge, Debbie instructs us on how to cross, explaining that it is important to keep the horse moving to prevent him from sitting down in the water. The flow is high because it is the rainy season, but the river is still shallow enough for the horses to cross. I am excited because this is the first time in a very long time that I've been on horseback. And we are riding into a river!

Titán and I cross last, and he steps gingerly over the rocky bottom. The other horses and their riders are already on the other bank when Titán and I make it across. Steady and sure-footed, he places one front hoof up onto the muddy side, but his rear hoof hits a loose rock. He trips and recovers quickly, but suddenly I am off his back and under the water. As I stand up, soaked head to toe and laughing, Titán looks back at me with embarrassment. I can see in his eyes and his bearing that he is apologetic and ashamed.

The horses are tied up, and we riders eat lunch and play in the river for a while. I find an eddy to sit in to enjoy a gentle water massage. From there I watch Juan José, one of the guides, as he plays. He climbs up into a tree, grabs hold of a hanging vine, and swings himself into a deep pool in the river.

The whole experience is otherworldly, so very far away from the life I am living back home. I feel joyful and totally relaxed.

When it is time to return to the cabin retreat, I climb onto Titán for the ride back. And that's when I clearly hear Titán speak. I don't mean that I interpret the look in his eyes, or read his body language, or assign some meaning to his actions. I actually hear him explain how bad he felt for failing to carry me safely. Not with words, of course, but through some other kind of communication, Titán is definitely speaking. It is as if something has opened inside of me making it possible for me to hear him.

All the way back from the river Titán continues talking, mostly about how he is concerned about whether I am okay, how humiliated he is, and how he has never before fallen with a rider let alone caused a rider to fall off his back. Just before arriving at the stable I hear him say,

By the way, I don't need any more training. Would you please tell that to Debbie?

I dismount, put away my helmet and bridle, wait for the other riders to leave, and then approach Debbie, Titán's owner.

"I don't know quite how to explain this," I say, "but Titán says to tell you he doesn't need any more training."

Debbie is taken aback.

"He said that? Isn't that interesting!" she exclaims.

I tell her all Titán had expressed, that he needs to have his way now and then, and that once and a while he'd appreciate a break. Furthermore, he insists that he knows exactly how to perform his job as a trail horse, and also as a therapeutic horse, and he is especially proud of his ability to take care of inexperienced riders.

Later that night over dinner, out of earshot of the other guests, Debbie tells me she had recently commented to the stableman that Titán might need to go back into training. They'd been discussing his habit of ignoring an inexperienced rider on his back, and of wandering off to eat, and they agreed that some refresher training might be in order. Apparently, Titán is aware of their intentions and was voicing his objections through me.

As a child, it never occurred to me to question the improbability of hearing a horse speak, or to consider communication between people and horses something out of the ordinary.

I had been keenly aware of the non-material realm since before the age of two, often seeing and hearing things that others around me did not. Once, a lady standing in the basement near the old coal furnace told me she had been killed in a deadly blaze, and warned me not to play with matches. Another time, I felt the presence of a young boy in a military

uniform who said nothing and never acknowledged my presence, but his anger was so permeating that I avoided a certain
bedroom entirely. A third spirit, milky-white, a woman, hov-
ered just outside my bedroom door. I was always aware of any
apparitions present in our family's homes.

At least from the time I could speak to tell of such encounters until my early teens, my perceptions extended beyond the
realm of physical reality. Understanding horses felt entirely
natural to me, but I didn't have words to explain it, so I never
told anyone or thought too hard about how or why it was happening. But that was many years ago, and I was young.

Now, I am a mature adult, who has raised a family and is
considered by many in my community to be a visionary and
a leader. In addition, I am at the height of a successful career
as a professor and a scholar. Those extra-perceptual senses
receded long ago under the responsibilities of adulthood, and
the demands of the shared, material reality. Hearing Titán, I
wonder what is happening, why it's happening now and how,
but never think to question what others will make of my horse
communication claim. So when Debbie and Steve, the cabin
retreat co-owners, seem anxious about what I might say to
their other guests, it dawns on me that this capacity could
be misconstrued or dismissed. It might even be feared and
rejected.

On the sixth day at the Arenal Volcano Cabin Retreat, I
oversleep and arrive at breakfast later than usual. I wolf down
two fried eggs from the farm, an English muffin, and a glass of
fresh blackberry juice. Then I go straight to the barn, guessing
that the horses will already be there. In fact, a number of them
are saddled up and waiting to go out on the trail. As I enter, I
notice a mare standing quietly to one side. She glances slowly

in my direction and then turns her head away. I wonder if she has something to say, so I approach her, knowing we have very little time before they will leave and hoping to speak with her without the other guests seeing me. I place my hand on her back and whisper into her ear, "You can trust me. Feel free to say what you want, and I will do my best to understand."

She forms an image in her mind of a man wearing a red shirt and holding some kind of implement in his hand. Sharing this with me, I can see it, though not with the kind of vision used to perceive the material world. Rather, it's like a faint impression. The image comes from her to me through a sense other than my eye's sight. I feel her disdain for this man. She is angry over some kind of violation he'd committed.

One of the guides comes up and politely explains to me that it is time for the rider to mount her. As I walk away, I still feel her sadness and wonder what exactly happened to her.

"I saw you with Suzy. Was she talking to you?" Debbie asks, approaching me as the horses and their riders are leaving the barn.

"Yes," I reply, and tell Debbie about what the mare said to me in the exchange.

"That must have occurred at her previous home," Debbie exclaims.

Later that afternoon, shortly after the horses return from the trail ride, I pass the barn on my way to dinner. Debbie, who is just leaving the main office, wonders if Gitana, another mare, will also talk to me. I am willing to try, even though I do not know what to expect or even what to do since horse communication is new to me.

GITANA

I can tell by the hesitation in Debbie's voice that she still has some doubts about my capacity to communicate with horses. But she also seems very concerned about her horse. Gitana, she explains, has been misbehaving in the herd, kicking other horses, and being obstinate when carrying tourists.

"I don't know what's wrong with her," Debbie says. "I am beginning to doubt that we can keep her." This is the first horse Debbie purchased, and the mare has lived at the cabin retreat since their arrival in Costa Rica. Debbie has grown attached to her and is pained by the prospect of having to sell her.

I follow Debbie into the stable where Gitana is standing back by the exit to the fields. We trudge through the muddy straw and stand by her side. Intuitively, I put my head close to her neck and explain in a whisper that I am there to listen.

She does not seem to respond, though her ears move back as I speak. For a few frustrating moments I wonder, "Whatever am I doing?" and begin to doubt my emerging capacity to hear horses speak. But I persist, telling Gitana, "It's really important that you share with me what is going on, because Debbie is thinking of getting rid of you."

Gitana turns her head and gently places her jaw on my shoulder. She stares at me with wide eyes. I tell her that I can understand her and ask that she please try to explain what is troubling her. She begins by telling me she is tired.

Debbie watches wide-eyed as Gitana and I connect. Gitana shares her sensations, emotions, and thoughts, and I interpret and translate those into spoken language. Debbie stands by in disbelief as I tell her that Gitana is feeling exhausted from the burdens of her role. Debbie says nothing, perhaps waiting to see if my communication will yield specific information.

"It's important that she have time alone, away from the herd," I explain. "She says she is exhausted from her job."

Only then does Debbie tell me that Gitana, a favored horse of hers, is one of the two lead-mares, which means she carries responsibility for the safety and protection of the entire herd.

Gitana directs my focus to her belly. I step back to get a better look at her underside. She is letting me know that something in that area of her body is worrying her.

"What's going on in there?" I ask, but Debbie has no idea, and doesn't know why I am asking. Then, in a vision, Gitana shows me a field where she wants to be left alone.

"Let's see if we can find the place she is showing me," I suggest, and Debbie agrees. We walk out of the stable, along a narrow path past the pig and chicken pens, searching for the field Gitana has shown me in the vision she shared with me.

"There it is!" I say, pointing when I recognize the pasture. It is located not far from the barn.

"Well, no wonder," Debbie replies as she opens the gate and leads us across the ridge by the field where Gitana has asked to be put. "Gitana keeps opening this gate and we keep having to reinforce it," she explains.

"Of course she does," I chuckle as we walk through. Debbie and I are both quiet as we stand looking over the field.

"You were talking to Gitana, and you understood what she was saying to you," she remarks, breaking the silence. "How are you able to do that?"

"I really don't know," I reply. "I am not even sure I am the one who's doing this."

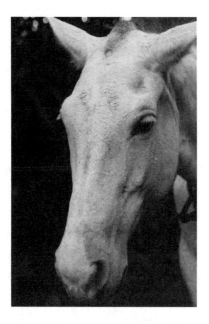

V

EQUINE ENCOUNTERS:
JUANO TEACHES

My respite at the cabin retreat was amazingly productive. While there I completed another edit of the novel manuscript, and yet I rested well. I came to feel much more at peace, and found myself more able to accept the impending finalization of my divorce. And I left Costa Rica with a wonderful sense of accomplishment. But what was I to make of my newfound ability to communicate with horses? How could I make sense of it? Had I hit my head when falling into the river off of Titán? Had I slipped into some kind of altered state? Admittedly, the previous year had been one of the most emotionally draining of my life, so perhaps the stress was affecting my mind. But if that were the case, how was I gleaning accurate information from each horse when I had no conventional way of knowing it?

After returning to the U.S., it was only a matter of time before I was buried once again under the responsibilities of my job. I was relatively new to the organization, having left my academic appointment to take the position just over a year before. So I was shocked when, only a few weeks after my return from vacation, the president of my organization announced that we were seriously in the red and that drastic changes were needed in order to stay afloat. So much for the peace of mind I'd acquired!

Shortly after I got back home, Debbie sent me an email message with news from Costa Rica. It turns out Gitana, the mare who wanted to have time away from the herd, had been pregnant when she and I communicated. That's what she was trying to show me. She lost the fetus shortly thereafter. Debbie instructed her stableman to put Gitana out alone in the pasture for a while every day, and she rapidly improved. There was no longer any need to consider selling her. I was happy to hear she was doing well, but so preoccupied with work that I could barely think about the horses. Instead, I had to consider whether or not to resign before it was too late to reclaim my university position. The new job was becoming less and less meaningful, a poor substitute for the richness of the classroom and the challenge and wonder of teaching college students.

One night in particular, filled with dismay over job and relationship issues, I fell asleep with a sense of loneliness I had never before experienced. Overcome with sorrow, I lamented the disintegration of my family and marriage and the loss of my home and the beautiful land that surrounds it. It seemed that being near Arenal, and especially spending time with the horses, had cracked the rigid wall of denial I had built around my grieving heart. The following morning, sitting in meditation, I prayed for a new romantic companion, not in pleading, silent supplication, but instead with emphatic, spoken

insistence. Before I knew it I was shouting out loud, scream-
ing with rage at God.

"Letting it all out" was cathartic, and successful. I met Bill
that same night, and soon came to recognize him as the very
companion I had prayed for. We enjoyed all kinds of activities together in the process of getting to know each other:
hiking, going to concerts, reading poetry, cooking meals, and
dancing. A few months passed, and an odd yet familiar feeling
came over me.

"I think I have to go back to Costa Rica," I told Bill.

I shared with him some of the details of my September
visit, and he was more than willing to accompany me to the
special place I'd discovered and to meet the horses who still
haunted my memories.

We arrive at the cabin retreat on an afternoon in early March,
six short months after my initial visit there. I excitedly take
Bill to see the horses. I am curious to know whether I will still
hear them speak. Debbie and her husband Steve, and Ronald,
one of the caretakers, are standing together just outside of the
stable with a horse I'd never seen before.

"Wow!" I exclaim. "Who is this?"

I approach the horse carefully. He is radiant, strong, and
incredibly beautiful, and holds his head high with self-confi-
dence. My heart rate increases as I move close enough to see
his eyes, but I am careful not to invade the personal space he
seems determined to maintain. He is a muscular auburn horse
with a dark blond mane and a white star on his forehead, and
he exudes dominance and power.

"This is Juano, our new stallion," Debbie says, as I stand
mesmerized by the presence of the horse. "He's a well-known

racing horse in Costa Rica and still holds the record for his performance in the quarter mile."

Juano lowers his head and extends his penis, licking and chewing as I open to our energy exchange.

"Look at his reaction to you!" Debbie says in surprise.

"He's stunning," I remark, as I study his form and scan for his emotional state. I feel that he senses much more about me than I do about him. Something is clearly happening between us.

"Hello, Juano," I say to him from a safe and respectful distance. I want to touch him, but refrain.

Debbie tells me that after his racing career ended, Juano was used for stud service and working with cattle. "His off-spring are heralded as the 'children of Juano,'" Debbie adds. His first owner sold him to Debbie. She bought him for impregnating mares and for trail rides and treks, though she allows only the most experienced guides to ride him.

That night I dream of Juano, though I don't recall the details. Most of what I remember when I awake in the morning is an image of his face and eyes looking in my direction, and an awareness that we've made a connection, a *vinculo* as Debbie says, Spanish for a bond between two souls. Juano is on my mind, and I am anxious to see him again. But he is not there when we go to find him. So after eating a typical Costa Rican breakfast of beans and rice, fresh farm eggs, fried plantains, and tropical fruits, Bill and I take off to enjoy a few tour-ist activities: hiking, soaking in thermal springs, and visiting the Arenal Volcano. Later that afternoon, after our return, we wander back up to the stable. Debbie is delighted we are here and asks if I am willing to talk with some more of her horses.

Together Debbie, Bill and I go into the stable. Some of the horses are present, but quite a few are either on trail rides or out in the field. Of each horse, one at a time, I ask very softly in a whisper, "Is there anything you'd like to say?"

TITÁN

Our first visit is with Titán, from whom I fell into the river, the horse who first spoke to me. He is definitely ready to speak again:

> *"You and I have talked before. This time I have only one thing to share and it's important for you to hear so that Debbie can know this. I have a sadness inside that comes from missing a horse that was in my life in the past. It was a mare. Maybe you humans see us as mating without love, but it's not true. We have love for one another. We have hearts, just like you do. We form bonds between us, also like you. I had formed a bond with that particular mare. She bore my child. Then, we were separated, all three of us. I think of her and of our child. We were a family, broken apart. Tell Debbie that when a new horse comes to join us here, that horse is probably in mourning for the horses they left behind, the ones they love and will miss. At least she should acknowledge that and let the horse know that she understands their pain. It will help them to move on. Humans ride us and then feel attachment. They feel they have bonded with us, and sometimes that is true. But you must understand that the most primary relationships for us are those we have with other horses. This is where our deepest bonds are formed. As for me, I will never see that mare again, but she is still in my heart. I don't blame anyone here. I simply want that to be known."*

Titán's father, Titáno, was a famous stallion and champion Costa Rican dancing horse. Titán's original owner had hoped that Titáno's son would also be a wonderful dancer, but Titán showed little desire to follow in his father's "hoof steps." His owners saw him as stubborn and willful but, believing in his bloodline, wouldn't give up trying to make him dance. But although Titán could dance if forced, he had no desire for it, and eventually his owners came to accept this. He was gelded and put into a pasture with a few mares. Then he was sold for $400 and the money was used to buy a wheelchair for the owner's handicapped son.

After Debbie acquired him, she put Titán to work as a trail horse for guests at the cabin retreat, and uses him in the *Vínculo con Caballo* therapeutic riding program. Handicapped children do very well on his back. He is a friendly horse and gentle with those who ride him. On a typical month during high season, he is on the trail almost every day. He is ridden by an average of 200 different people per year. Children, in particular, are his favorite and are drawn to Titán.

MR. BIG

I meet Mr. Big for the first time on this visit. Yet it is as if he's been waiting for my return to the cabin retreat:

"There is much I have to say. Let's begin with the fact of my anger, though that feeling didn't originate with me. But this I will explain a bit later. First, I want to inform you that horses, like people, can grow and change. And like people, we are always trying to improve ourselves, and to gain control over our minds.

I think you should be proud of me, because despite all the anger I feel inside, and all the hurt I carry around in my heavy heart, I am working hard to release and transform it. Would you say I am doing a good job?

Before I came here, I lived with a very angry man. He had so much anger he didn't know what to do, so he threw it all on me. His words were mean and he called me stupid and worthless. He used his whip to thrash my back and butt, trying to release what he could no longer contain. And what do you think happened to his anger? Well, it went right inside of me, that's what.

Why, you ask? Because I allowed it to do so. That's what we horses do.

We take in whatever you humans bring to us. If you bring fear, we take in your fear. If you bring joy, we take in your joy. If you bring anger with you, that's what we will feel. These feelings we take in remain more yours than our own because we release

37

our own feelings almost as soon as they arise. Yes, some of us hold grudges, but most of us don't. Usually, we forgive.

I am able to help, but I also need help. Though I am improving and working hard to release this pain, I ask you to let me know that you love me and that I am truly lovable. Touch me in loving ways. Speak to me in loving tones. I will heal.

"What in the world happened to Mr. Big?" I ask once we are out sight and earshot of him.

Debbie explains that she had been looking for new horses for the retreat, and a man in the community needed to pay his hardware store bill and was interested in selling a few of his horses to raise the money. Debbie tried out several, but when she mounted Mr. Big she said immediately, "I want this one." The man replied, "No, you don't want that one. Try another." But Debbie insisted.

As it turns out, my interpretation of what Mr. Big shared with me was accurate. Debbie knew what had happened. A previous owner, someone Debbie did not know personally, had tortured him. She was told that this man had tied Mr. Big's head to his tail to break him of the habit of running back to the barn.

"You can see the scars right on his face," she says.

Several months after my first conversation with Mr. Big, one of the horsemen, Erick, commented on how much happier the horse seemed to be, full of energy and enthusiasm. "He's so different!" he exclaimed to Debbie. "How do you explain the change in him?" Debbie told Erick about Mr. Big's conversation with me and how, as a result, Mr. Big finally knew he had a place in the world where he was appreciated and understood. Having had a chance to reveal his truth, to express all the heaviness that had been in his heart and mind, he'd been released into joy. Where in the past only an experienced rider could handle him, as he was extremely sensitive to individuals with anxiety or nervousness, today he can be ridden by anyone and is used regularly as a therapy horse.

DORADO

Debbie leaves to check on a few matters in the office and Bill returns to the cabin to rest, but I elect to remain in the stable to see what more I can learn. Dorado is a golden-hued gelding, as his name suggests. He has been watching me the whole time as I speak with the other horses. I invite him to talk, but it is quite a while before he opens up to me and responds. When he finally does, he has a great deal to say:

"Why do you ask that I share with you about who I am inside? Do you not see that just by looking at me? I am healthy and happy. I have a very good life here. Don't ask me to open up and spill out feelings that will cause needless sadness or sorrow. The last thing that I want is any more of that.

If you must glean something from me so that you feel that your work has been done, then share this: I was given wonderful training and care. I feel great gratitude to my "owner." Yes, my owner sent me here to this place, but it is good for me here, and I am well. So stop waiting for me to give more information. Do your job and just tell him that.

I see that you are still waiting around, as if I might have more to say. You want to know who I am? Who I really am inside? I am a horse with great love for my owner. To him I will be forever grateful. Let's be clear, though, about ownership of a horse. It has little to do with the exchange of money and papers. A horse cannot be owned at all. No, though you may think otherwise, a horse *chooses to make a connection of love and compassion, of devotion and trust, and that choice is not based on who has the formal agreements or on who has paid whom for the trade. I will tell you about ownership. It belongs to one who made a sacrifice on my behalf and wants only for me to be well. Unlike so many so-called owners, who are selfishly looking for the love of a horse, the man I consider my owner made a great sacrifice to assure that I would be well taken care of.*

And I am.

On another matter, know that I understand what the humans around me are saying about me and at times even about the others. It's not that I recognize your words. Language is not a capacity that I have. I understand what you say even before the words form on your lips. The meaning flows directly from your mind to mine. I even understand what you do not say, what you are afraid to say, or are unable to articulate. So, do know that I am listening. I am listening deeply and well.

You ask about my work with humans that are handicapped. I will explain. I recall one rider in particular, someone whose brain was not right.

By now, Debbie has returned and I share with her what Dorado has told me so far. She surmises that he must be referring to a woman with autism who had recently ridden him.

To you, she does not seem to have the capacity to understand human communication clearly. Here is what you may not understand: I, and most horses like me, are able to sense such gaps. And then, when and if we choose to do so, we can help by filling those gaps from inside of our own beings so that, at least during the time that person is with us, they no longer feel deficient.

Here is something else. When humans are unable to do their own work to release and dispel their own pain and suffering, we horses are able to support the process of their healing.

Exercising that capacity, which we are born with, is natural to us.

We are compassionate creatures who have the desire to help others to heal. Most of us are eager to make this kind of connection, and feel honored when we sense a change for the better because of what we do.

But know this: horses who are mistreated, disrespected, or dishonored, can and do lose that natural ability. Not only can they no longer help in healing, they will need to be healed themselves.

Not realizing that Dorado has finished, I continue to lean against the post looking at him.

Have I not yet said enough? Still you stand and wait. What, exactly, are you waiting around for? I have told you already that I am fine. . . .

"Are you certain there's nothing else you wish to say?" I inquire.

. . . All right, then, since you ask, I do have one request. Let me be ridden again by my owner. May we have an entire day? Let us run across fields, along the riverbanks, over mountains and along the wooded trails. I want for us to be together again, alone, a horse and his owner out on the land.

I thank Dorado for speaking with me and let Debbie know of his request. Then Debbie shares with me the whole of his story:

Chito, a man from a neighboring farm and one of Debbie's part-time guides, had acquired Dorado as a two-year-old. Half Quarter Horse and half Arabian, Chito trained him from the beginning. Dorado became well known in the area for rodeo performances, cattle work, and barrel racing. Eventually, he earned championship status in Costa Rica. When his days on the rodeo circuit were over, Dorado was put on the market and brought the excellent price of over four thousand dollars. But the new owner couldn't make the second payment, and Dorado was returned to Chito, who offered to let Debbie use him for trail rides in exchange for room and board.

Once settled in at the cabin retreat, Dorado quickly found a secure position within the herd, working as both a trail horse and therapeutic horse. But soon after his arrival, another buyer offered Chito an even higher price for Dorado. Chito saw how well Dorado worked with inexperienced, nervous tourists and also with handicapped children, and realized that this work was becoming an integral part of Dorado's life and purpose. He felt Dorado belonged with Debbie, as he was content, well cared for, and loved. Recognizing that Dorado's happiness was much more valuable than money, he sold him to Debbie for $1300.

He certainly seems happy to me.

BEAUTY

"My goodness!" I exclaim. "What a gorgeous horse!" The grace and stature of the mare is striking, and she immediately draws my attention and interest.

"Oh, that's Beauty," Debbie says affectionately.

I take a seat on the cement half-wall in the middle of the stable, which provides just the right vantage point from which to observe the lovely horse. It isn't long before Beauty walks over to me.

"Hello, Beauty," I speak, as she comes up next to me. I sense she has come in from the pastures because she wants to talk. Without any further prompting, she begins to communicate:

> *That's a good name for me, "Beauty." Everyone always says how striking I am, with my nearly black coat and the contrasting white star that descends from my forehead down to my mouth. People can't help but touch me when they see me, rubbing and petting my mane and my sides while commenting on my stunning looks. I don't mind. It feels good to be seen in this way. But I wonder if they see who I am, inside I mean, the way that I see them. For example, can they see how much I worry about the other horses, and that I worry even more about the people who ride me? Maybe worry isn't the right word. Let's just say they are often on my mind.*
>
> *I would say that even more important than my physical characteristics, at least to me, is my capacity to feel the emotions of people and other horses. It's a trait I received from my mother, who received it from her mother before her. I am able to sense things about a person not so much from what they look like, but more from how they feel on the inside. It's in my blood, but it's also just the kind of horse I am. If a visitor rides me even one time, I can tell something about how they feel about themselves and their life. More often than not, I sense that they feel bad about themselves.*
>
> *Many humans are sad and afraid. They are afraid that they are not good enough or that they aren't doing enough. However, I sense on a deeper level that they are afraid and confused because*

they no longer know who they are, where they belong, or what it means to be living. Not like me. I know that I am a horse and I like that I am a horse. I also know that I belong right here.

With many riders, I make a bond and we feel a connection to each other. This is easier to do with children, because even the sick ones seem to be sure of themselves.

With the adults there is also a connection, though it has a more urgent feeling to me. I am open, wide open, and they notice that and feel how I sense them inside and out. That makes them open up to me. I feel that many of them are really heavy. I don't mean their weight on my back. I mean that they are heavy on the inside. When I sense that they are feeling bad, I want to heal them. So when they climb out of the saddle and walk on the ground again, everything inside and outside of them feels lighter, and they remember who they are.

It works, most of the time, except when it's time to say goodbye and some of them get sad all over again. I get sad too, because it's not just a one-way thing. My sadness is different from theirs, *though. What's hard for me, really hard, is that once they start to feel that they are really alive, they have to leave. I sense they feel they still need to be with me. They are afraid that they won't be able to carry themselves as lightly as I have carried them.*

But they can.

Oh, since we're communicating like this, may I please have a crunchy snack? I have been eating hay all day, but it's the crunchy stuff that I want.

Debbie steps out for a bit while Beauty and I continue to converse. "I think Beauty wants a carrot," I exclaim when she returns, "as a treat for having spoken with me."

"That's odd. Beauty's never eaten carrots before," Debbie replies. Yet she hops on the four-wheeler and goes to the kitchen, returning with carrots in hand. Beauty isn't interested at all and turns away when the carrots are offered.

"I guess I misunderstood," I admit. "I just know she was asking for 'crunchy.'"

"Crunchy! Is that what she said?" Debbie asks.

"Well, yes, to be exact. I just figured she must have meant carrots," I answer.

"No, if she said 'crunchy' then she meant *concentrado!*"

Debbie disappears around the corner into the tack room, returning with a bucket of concentrated horse food. Beauty stuffs her nose inside the container and gobbles up the food. Debbie laughs as Beauty enjoys the treat.

"She never seems to get enough of this," she says. She thinks it is funny that Beauty figures she has somehow earned the special snack by speaking with me.

This is a very important lesson for me, not to dismiss what I hear in favor of my own assumptions and ideas. In order to truly understand what the horses are saying, I have to trust and accept what I sense is being said. This is the first of many such lessons.

As Beauty finishes her snack, Debbie shares more of the horse's story. Before coming to the cabin retreat, Beauty lived on a farm in a nearby province. She was a brood mare (a female horse used for breeding) that had been left to run free in the pastures. Her hoofs were big, unkempt, paddle-like, and full of fungus because she lived in a swampy area and often needed to swim between pastures to graze. Debbie had seen her running with her baby, and knew that Beauty was special. She purchased both mother and foal. But once weaned, her foal was sent back to its original owner.

At the cabin retreat, Beauty bore another baby, but it died when it was two weeks old. Two years later, Beauty delivered a healthy foal.

STELLA

Stella is the bright-eyed and energetic three-year-old daughter of Gitana. She was conceived, born, and imprinted (her mental process molded to human interaction) at the cabin retreat. I place my hand on the top of her head and ask if she is interested in talking with me. She seems receptive, though she has relatively little to say:

I am still young. That means I need to be free. I see the mares here, how they have such power and responsibility, how they care for and protect their young while directing the others as well. I, too, want such status. I want to rise to the top. Not yet, though, if it means I must bear young. I am not ready for that. I still want to enjoy my youth and the freedom to be that it allows.

Through your touch, you have felt my mind and sensed the complexity of my thinking. So you know of my capacity to understand multiple layers of meanings. I understand what it will mean to become the one who will lead the herd. I know that, one day, that will be me. For now, let me be, and keep the stallions away from me.

I realize I am feeling fatigued. Listening to horses requires me to focus and sense in ways I am not accustomed to. It may have something to do with the energetic connection needed to maintain the flow of communication. I say goodbye, but Debbie seems disappointed; there are horses with whom I have not yet communicated. I promise to return.

Back at the cabin I join Bill out on the porch. Together we reflect on the day's curious events as we gaze across the valley to the volcano. What does this all mean? Why have I been drawn back to this place? Is there a particular way in which I am meant to use this gift? I go to the bedroom to lie down and try to nap, but am unable. With more horses still to meet, and so much more to learn from them, I am soon up and on my way back to visit the horses grazing out in the field.

CORTESSA

Reaching the top of the driveway, I notice a horse standing just behind the fence at the upper ledge of the pasture. I move across the grass to the barbed wire enclosure.

"Hi there," I call, hoping that she will turn and approach me. But she doesn't move. Why do I think she will respond to me, or that I will be significant to her in any way? Who do I think I am? What do I think I am doing? I am beginning to doubt myself, but I persist.

"Don't you want to come over here and have a chat?" My ego has been fed by my prior successful exchanges with the other horses, and I've grown proud of my newfound capacity to hear the horse's voices.

Two women in uniform walk by, making their way along the rocky driveway from the kitchen toward the town road.

"*Hola*," I say as they pass by.

"*Buenos tardes*," they return cordially. What must these two be thinking? Here I am, a North American woman with little experience of horses, standing by the fence and talking to one. I start to return to the cabin, thinking it will be best to step away from the entire affair for a while. Debbie is on her way back from the dining area when we happen to meet.

"It looks like you were talking to Cortessa," she says.

"Not really," I fret.

"Why don't we see if she'll come into the stable? Then maybe she will talk."

Ronald, the stableman, grabs a lead rope to get her. Cortessa follows him willingly. And she definitely has something to say:

"For some reason, I guess I know why, they hold me back from participating like the others. I like being with the people who visit and I don't mind at all when people ride on my back. But sometimes, more often than not, I get in trouble for something I've done, like licking all the time from the empty feed bin when I am supposed to be eating hay. I think they think I am uncontrollable. I'm not. Well, maybe to them I am, but I don't mean to be. I really do want to please them, especially the woman called Debbie. She's good to me. She takes care of me and I sometimes get scared she'll send me away.

You see, I'm different. I know that, only I can't exactly explain how. Sometimes, when I am riding along in the group with the others and there is someone on my back, I get a little distracted and suddenly I get agitated. My mind wants to focus on whatever has gotten my attention and at the same time, the person who is riding me is trying to get me to focus on what they want me to do. Well, maybe I just can't, not then at least. Maybe I just have to keep my mind on whatever has attracted me, like the sound of the river, or the mud up ahead, or whatever is flying around the tail of the horse in front of me. Or maybe it's the gravel stuck in my hoof, or the smell of guava on a nearby tree, or the way the sound of the metal bit on the halter clangs in my ears. In truth, sometimes I don't know what it is that has distracted me; only that having a rider on my back at that particular moment is an annoyance. I understand. It's scary for a rider when I suddenly rear back, or begin turning this way and that. It's just that I get distracted.

When I can't ride the trail with the guides and they put me out in the field, I feel as though I am being punished. I think maybe someone will come and take me away from this place, from my home and my herd, and then the woman called Debbie will find a better horse who she can depend on to do things right.

There's one more thing for you to know. I may be a little different, but I like people a lot. And also, I will be a really good mother to my babies. So don't worry at all about that."

As Cortessa and I speak, Debbie stands close by, amazed at what I am hearing. Cortessa's insight has moved her. Once the communication is complete and we walk away, Debbie explains something about Cortessa's background.

Her father was a thoroughbred racer, and she had been bred to race. She was about two years old when Debbie brought her home to the cabin retreat. Early in her training, it was discovered that Cortessa had issues with "collection" and with moving her head and limbs in unison. She quickly unraveled and was difficult to control. Though her trainers continued to work with her and taught her the basics of carrying a rider, she remained flighty and, at times, unpredictable.

At the first opportunity, Debbie and her crew took Cortessa to a local horse race held at an old airplane landing strip. Juan José, one of her trainers, elected to ride that day as her jockey. As soon as the race began, Cortessa took off at an incredible speed, barreling down the track flanked by one other horse. At the end of the course, in the slowdown area, she spotted a familiar stallion. Suddenly she turned off the course and jumped over a 4x4 car to reach her equine

friend. Juan José lost control, Cortessa's jump fell short, and she landed on the car's hood. Juan José was slammed into the windshield. Thankfully, neither was hurt, but after that event it was decided that she would have to undergo retraining. Meanwhile, no tourists would be riding her.

SUZY (1)

A horse who I think I recognize from my first visit, is watching intently from the other side of the aisle as I am communicating with Cortessa.

"Who is that?" I ask, just to make sure this is the same horse I think I remember. Debbie clarifies that it is, indeed, Suzy.

We move over to where she is standing. "Is there anything you'd like to talk about?" I ask. Her answer is immediate:

"Yes. I want you to thank them for noticing that I was ready to accept the stallion. It was a wonderful, fulfilling experience. Not like the last time I was taken to the stallion." (11 months later, Martha was born.)

Suzy shows me the same image as before, only with more details this time. Held in a space between her mind and mine, I make out the faint shadows of a riding ring. A man wearing red grabs on to her tightly, and holds a mechanical clamp in his hand. A stallion mounts her. I feel it to be a violent encounter. Something inside me knows just what she feels.

""I wasn't ready," she says. "I wasn't ready," she repeats.

"What is she talking about?" I ask Debbie.

Debbie explains that Suzy was purchased from a neighbor who lives near the retreat. The owner had purchased her pregnant with an Arabian foal as he wanted a half-Arabian and half-Criollo horse for endurance racing. Once Suzy gave birth, she was no longer of use to him. Debbie bought Suzy

from him for three hundred dollars, intending to use her as a trail horse. When Suzy first came to the cabin retreat, she was very difficult to handle, and would try to bite or kick anyone who touched or approached her from the left side.

Debbie surmises that Suzy's comment about not being ready could be in reference to an experience she had the year before. They'd sent her to a Quarter Horse breeder who owned stallions from a well-known bloodline, imported from the United States.

"We thought Suzy was in heat and so we had her transported to the farm," Debbie explains. "But she wasn't, and she wouldn't accept the stallion. The veterinarian gave her a hormone shot to speed the maturation of an ovum. He told the ranch hands to wait three days and then to put the stallion with her, whether she accepted him or not. Her legs were tied so she wouldn't be able to kick the valuable Quarter Horse."

This is more than I can bear to hear. No wonder Suzy told me she wasn't ready. How could she have been? It is time for me to take a break.

JUANO

The next day, Debbie kindly arranges for Bill and me to take a horseback ride to a waterfall with two of her guides, Enrique and Chito. After a wonderful breakfast, we meet the guides in the barn where they are saddling up horses for us— four horses, including Juano! With much excitement, I head straight for him and announce how happy I am to see him again. I place my hand on the side of his neck and am about to give him a hug. That's when I feel myself being stared at, and look up to see that a horse on the other side of the barn is looking at me in dismay.

Debbie walks into the barn.

"Who is this horse I am standing next to right now?" I call to her. With people, and apparently with horses too, I tend to have trouble connecting a familiar face with a name.

"Oh, that's Mr. Big," she clarifies.

I am mortified. I step away from Mr. Big and walk gingerly over to greet the horse I'd intended to shower with affection. As I approach Juano, he turns away from me.

"Juano, I am so sorry," I say, moving toward his head. "I can't believe I confused you with Mr. Big." My intention to reconnect with him is foiled.

"Please forgive me," I ask.

He shifts himself around until his rear end is in front of my chest, rejecting me in a way that is unexpected and insulting.

"Really, Juano? Come on, now!" I exclaim, walking back to his side.

No response. It feels as if I don't exist to him.

I decide to make a last attempt to square things with Juano. I stand close to his head and whisper, "I mean it. I really am sorry. I apologize." But Juano wants nothing to do with me. I can read in his eyes that my mistaking him for Mr. Big has deeply offended him.

We mount our horses with Bill riding Mr. Big and I on Titán. With Enrique riding Juano and Chito on Dorado, the eight of us spend the better part of the day riding over hills where cattle graze, along narrow ridges, down steep slopes, through rainforests, across rivers, and through wide-open pastures. At midday we tie the horses up under a shady grove and hike into the forest, over a cliff, and down to a 30-foot waterfall. There we eat a bag lunch packed for us by the cabin retreat staff, and then swim in the deep pool formed below by the water cascading into the river. The setting is Eden-like.

On our return, we cross a wide meadow where we stop to take in the beauty around us. Enrique lies back in his saddle and looks up at the sky.

"*Pura vida!*" he exclaims, using the Costa Rica expression for a good, pure life. We chat with our two guides for a while about their lives and what it was like to grow up in rural Costa Rica. As we prepare to get going again, something inspires Bill to lean forward and kick Mr. Big, which sends him into a gallop. In a flash, Juano takes off, too. It is stunning to watch Juano's speed, agility, and grace as he effortlessly passes Mr. Big up the hillside.

"You have to warn me before you do that!" Enrique tells Bill after they stop. Both horses are dripping with sweat, their hearts pounding. Enrique had hardly had a moment to sit upright and prepare for a race. I suspect that Juano's act was both instinctual and intentional: first, there was no way he was going to let the horse I'd mistaken him for surpass him in any way! Besides that, he was still a record-holding racer in Costa Rica and he was not about to let any other horse outrun him.

The following day, Bill and I watch as the horses are prepared for another day of trail riding. Juano is there again. I go to greet him, hoping that he has forgiven me. Still he ignores me, making me feel invisible.

CARETTO
(the horse formerly known as Flaco)

On our last day, Debbie takes us to a nearby *"finca"* (farm) where her former employee, Juan José resides. During our visit to there, I notice a horse on the far side of a fenced corral. I feel a powerful attraction to him and know that it is very important that we make a connection. "Flaco?" Debbie questions when I ask to speak with this particular horse. "That one is Juan José's," she explains. (Flaco means "skinny" in Spanish.) Juan José is baffled, yet he and everyone else leave me alone to talk to the horse.

It takes perhaps five or ten minutes before Flaco comes close enough to be touched. When he finally reaches the fence, I reach over the top and place my hand on his side. Shortly thereafter, he speaks:

> *I am glad to be here now, but I am still very angry. I know that the man who had me before was intending to kill me. I worked hard for him. And then, when I didn't do as he dreamed, when he stopped believing in me, and when I got sick, he had no use for me anymore. He thought I would be the next great champion, like my father before me. I tried. I really tried. I worked hard for him, and I was loyal to him. But no matter what I did, he didn't care. He pushed me harder and harder even though he knew I was sick. I don't deserve what he did. All he cared about was money and fame.*
>
> *Now, here, they have changed my name. But my name is not Flaco. I may be sickly and weak, but I do not deserve that name. I am not who I appear to be on the outside. Inside I am still powerful and strong. Inside I am a great horse.*

I share with Juan José what his horse has told me. He listens carefully and receptively. In fact, his response is emotional. Close to tears, Juan José takes Flaco to a private spot in the stable where he apologizes to the horse. He looks straight into the horse's soul and recognizes who he is. Immediately, he changes the horse's name back to Caretto. He has never been called Flaco since then.

On the ride back to the cabin retreat, Debbie tells me all about Juan José. He'd originally worked for Steve and Debbie. During his employment with them, he began to develop skills in the Parelli method, an approach based on the philosophy of natural horsemanship practiced at their retreat. Juan José has devoted his entire adult life to the care and training of horses. When he first laid eyes on Caretto, the original owner was no longer willing to care for him. In fact, he had a gun to his head. Juan José was horrified and asked him not to pull the trigger. He saw great potential in Caretto. But he hadn't the money to purchase him, so Juan José offered his time and skills in exchange for the horse. He trained the man's other horses until he had earned enough credit to finally take his beloved horse back to his home, where he re-named him Flaco because he was so unhealthy and weak. Breaking all traditions, and thwarting his family's hopes and expectations, Juan José invested his time and effort not in the purchase of cattle and land, but instead in a sickly horse that otherwise would have been destroyed.

Bill and I prepare to leave for the airport, our Costa Rican adventure at an end, and we load our bags into the rented 4x4. It's time to say goodbye to our hosts Steve and Debbie.

"Thank you for everything," I offer.

"Yes, it's been great," adds Bill.

"Rosa, you really have to write about all this," Debbie insists as she bids us farewell. "People must know what we are learning from these horses. It could change the way horses are treated."

I am not inclined to follow her suggestion, as I am already under contract to write a book in my field of scholarship. Furthermore, I am still feeling insecure about my new clairaudient ability. Did I actually hear horses speaking?

Bill and I get in the car to drive away but my heart still aches over Juano. I see that he is very close by, tied up alone in the barn. So I hop out, attempting once again to seek his forgiveness.

"Please, Juano. Why can't you forgive me?" I ask as I approach him. (How odd to be talking to a horse as if he were a boyfriend who'd decided to break up with me!) "I have apologized to you three times for confusing you with another horse. I just don't know what else to do."

This time Juano replies:

You stroll into this barn full of pride, thinking of yourself as a horse communicator. Not yet you aren't. Not until you realize that we are individuals, who have been given, and know, our own names. We also have distinctive personalities, physical qualities, and feelings. So don't come waltzing in here as if you are God's gift to horses, expecting us to want to talk to you, if you haven't even the decency to recognize who we are.

Juano had become my teacher. And the first lesson he'd taught me was respect.

VI

EQUINE ENCOUNTERS.
OPENING TO BEAUTY

A year passes. I return to my university teaching position and, as luck would have it, am offered the opportunity to participate in a study-abroad program aboard a ship that is embarking from Costa Rica. I'd be going back once again. Bill was busy with work, so I'd make this next trip alone. I left the U.S. three days early to allow for a brief visit with my friends at the Arenal cabin retreat.

News of my communications with the horses had spread in the small Costa Rican community of Monterrey and beyond. The horsemen, the veterinarian, and the cabin retreat employees were all aware of it. Some had reacted with apprehension, suspicious of my abilities, while others were afraid that I might be reading *their* minds, too, and didn't want to come too close to me. Most were simply doubtful, especially those who'd been around horses most of their lives. At least a few thought I was plainly "*loco.*" But there were those who were open-minded and curious, and willing to observe and determine for themselves the authenticity of my claim.

It was my third visit to the cabin retreat, but I remained unsure whether the horses would speak to me again. Could I still hear the horses whisper, or were my previous experiences an anomaly? I told Debbie I would follow up with the same horses I'd met in the early spring, to see how they were doing and find out whether any of them had any new concerns. But first, I wanted to see Juano again, the stallion who taught me about horses' deserving that I respectfully know their names. And so before breakfast, very early in the morning on the day after I arrive, I head up to the stable. Juano is not there, though Debbie is.

"Hi!" she calls out as she approaches me.

"Good morning, Debbie" I reply. "Where is my friend Juano?"

She explains that, because he is a stallion, he has to be kept separate from the rest of the herd. She directs me down the driveway to a smaller barn and pasture where he is kept.

"Hello, beautiful boy," I say as I approach, stopping a few feet away from him. He turns in my direction. "I am so happy to be with you again. Are you willing to speak with me?" Clearly, he remembers me and is quite interested in speaking:

> *"When you look at me, know who I am and see me as the horse that I am. Learn my name and remember it. I am Juano, a great stallion and father to many horses.*
>
> *Suffice it to say that I am strong, very strong. In fact, people all over know of my strength and power. Horses know of it, too. I am more than that, though. I have feelings and keen senses, and I notice all kinds of things about people.*
>
> *When I run, and I do run fast, even ahead of the wind, it's exhilarating for me. I like to share that with a rider who is not*

afraid, one who, like me, enjoys the feeling of being completely free. It's hard to find such a one as that, one who can ride me without needing to demonstrate his power at my expense. This is why it's best that I am left alone most of the time.

My power can overwhelm an inexperienced rider, and I have little patience for the weakness of horses or people and especially those who try to control and contain me.

This is how my impatience shows up: I simply demonstrate who is in charge. Don't try to outrun or outsmart me. Even though it may seem that I have submitted to you, it is you who has actually submitted to me.

I am more powerful than you humans will ever be. You may train, rope, and contain me, but I will remain a force of nature. Given that, why not simply be with me?

If I am to live with humans and be ridden and cared for by them, I know that I need to follow their rules and obey their commands. Fair enough, but it can be tiresome. I'd rather move when and how I want. Still, there are times when I am content to just go along under the lead of a human. I can even play your horse training games. But my will can never be broken. So how about if we just respect one another?

If you spend time with me, remember to say hello, and also goodbye. If you are leaving this place and you may not be coming back, I need to know that so an adjustment can be made in my heart. I take our connection seriously.

Just before Bill and I had driven away the previous year, I had found and spoken to Juano. But I'd neglected to tell him I was leaving. I was absorbed in wanting his forgiveness and did not consider it important to say goodbye to him. He is scolding me for this, and rightly so.

Juano seems different this time, perhaps a bit sad. "Are you alright?" I ask. "Is something bothering you?" He continues.

Yes, but it's something I'd rather not think about right now, so I will say it only once, and briefly. But do not share this with others. It is a private matter between us. I sense my power weakening. I am afraid it will not remain strong in me. Soon I must pass it along to my sons.

I do not understand quite what he means. But I intend to keep his confidence.

That afternoon I go with Debbie to greet a few of the horses I have not yet met. Ronald, the stableman, spends almost his entire day around the horses, feeding them, changing their shoes, washing them down, giving them medicine, mucking the stables, keeping the tack room organized, and preparing the horses for riders. A reserved, soft-spoken man, he sits by unobtrusively and watches as I connect with each horse. According to Ronald, most of what I interpret from each horse fits that horse uniquely. Hearing this helps me to trust myself more and to stay open to the process unfolding within me.

J.R.

J.R. is the first horse I speak with on this day.

> *I want to know why I am not being chosen to father offspring. It feels like I am being punished. Why do you keep moving me from one place to another, separated from the other horses, with no one for company except Conan or Bonito? It's really confusing to me. Can you please explain what's going on? Juano is a stallion. You use him for breeding the mares. You never use me. Have I done something wrong?*

Suzy's son, J.R. was bred, born, and imprinted at the cabin retreat. Until he came into sexual maturity, he was an amazingly gentle horse. But his increasing testosterone became a potential danger to other horses. He was separated from the herd and put with a gelding for company, to avoid an accidental insemination of one of the mares. Debbie's intention is to have him castrated, because only one stallion can be handled at the retreat. I suggest to her that we explain that to J.R. before the operation.

CONAN

Conan seems to be ignoring us as we move through the stables. When we stop beside him and I invite him to speak, his eyes open wide with surprise.

> *Really? Really? You can hear me? You can understand? I need to process this information. I am accustomed to observing humans, listening to humans, doing what humans say, but I have never, ever been asked by a human to share my feelings and thoughts. I am not used to this. How can I trust that this is really what it seems?*
>
> *Hmm. Wow.*
>
> *I don't know what to say or how to act. All of my life I've been mute around humans, because none of them seemed to care about anything I might have to say. No one ever attempted to ask me what was on my mind. Most of us horses are that way. We just shut down inside when we are around people, so most of the time we don't even know how we feel or what we think because we have to hide those feelings away in order to keep on going. We assume that no one really cares about what we have to say anyway. Most*

people just want us to follow orders, or make them feel better, or keep them company. What we really want is to communicate in just this way. That's what it takes to form a real relationship, even with a horse.

We are born with the capacity to express ourselves, to listen and to communicate. It's so natural. It's who we are: the great communicators of the animal kingdom.

I don't know much about other animals, but I would guess that horses are the most communicative of the mammals, maybe even more so than those annoying primates that hang around screeching in the trees. As far as communication goes, you are more like us than you are like them. We live right here with you, on the ground.

We have been around you for so long that we have learned to recognize your gestures, interpret your expressions, and understand your languages. Do you understand what I am saying when

I tell you that it is part of the nature of domesticated horses to communicate with each other and also with humans? I have never even seen a wild horse, so I'm only guessing, but I don't think they share our capacity to communicate with humans. In order to adapt to being around you humans, living in your shelters, eating your foods, carrying you on our backs, we've had to adjust and learn your ways. It's how we survive, mentally. Otherwise, we'd go crazy. Some of us do anyway.

Wow. I can hardly stop the flow of thoughts from myself to you. I have been mute for so long, I can hardly contain myself. Who are you that you can do this? You look like everyone else, but I sense you can understand me. I had heard about you from some of the others, the ones who knew you from before. They sensed you were coming back here. They felt on several occasions that you were going to come back, but something prevented you, and this time they knew you almost didn't come until Debbie made it possible for you. We are grateful to her that she helped you come because, as you can imagine, there is a lot that we hold inside. We know we can share our feelings with you, and it's important to us to do so.

I have been watching you communicate with the other horses, but I waited until I was sure that you could actually understand us. Lots of people talk to us, all the time. But nearly all adults have forgotten how to listen, not just to horses but to each other, too. So we don't even bother sharing with them what is going on, at least not the really personal matters. Sure, the humans can read our body language, and they are pretty good at figuring things out from there—our expressions are pretty obvious. Some, like Debbie, can go a little deeper and feel what we feel. We hope that soon she will be able to understand us like you do.

Oh, something else about Debbie, and all humans, in fact. She does things to us, trying out new things, like the shoes and the games. We go along even when it's uncomfortable because we trust her.

You see, the first and strongest sense we have about humans is their intentions. Only those with good intentions earn our trust.

We know Debbie's intentions for us are good. She has a good heart. So we go along with her new ideas, even if we think they are silly. Sometimes we laugh about it. (Yes, horses laugh and we have a sense of humor, and we like to play pranks on people, and there are other things we do that I may not tell you, ever!) We are devoted to her because of her intentions. They are pure.

Ronald is another one we like and trust. We are spending a lot of our energy and effort on teaching him things. He is learning well, but still has so much to learn. We hope he stays here because he has great potential. He is willing to learn, so we are patient with him.

Debbie has raised the issue of putting heavy people on my back. I am not complaining. She brought it up, and I appreciate that. And yes, I would like some relief from the pain, but please don't give me any drugs during my workday. Hold off until the end of the day, right before I go to sleep. And preferably, don't give me anything that makes me feel like I am not myself.

"Conan the Barbarian" is anything but a barbarian. He was purchased for trail rides to carry less experienced riders. A big, heavy Quarter Horse, mild-mannered and easy-going, Debbie sees him as a good fit for the retreat. Little is known about his past other than that he was used for cattle and other farm work.

PICA

When I approach her, I mistakenly assume Pica will be interested in speaking. Instead, she is agitated. All she says is:

Don't bother, because I am not listening to you.

As suggested in the colloquial expression, "Talk to the hand," she lets me know she has no interest at all in speaking with me. Still, I stand there and attempt to stroke her. She lays her ears back and snarls.

What are you looking at? And don't presume you can just reach out and touch me. How would you like it if you were tied to a post, unable to move, and a horse put his face in front of you and stared at you like you are staring at me right now?

That is that for my conversation with Pica. Afterwards, Debbie explains that she was born in the pasture and had roamed freely without human contact for the first three years of her life. She is used as a trail horse and works well, even with children, but was difficult to train and does not like to be in the company of humans when given a choice.

Since our seemingly inauspicious encounter, Debbie tells me, Pica is changing little by little and warming up to human interactions.

SUZY (2)

From across the narrow pathway between the two sides of the stable, a gray and white mare named Suzy stares directly at me. We'd talked before about the intrusive breeding that was forced upon her. Now she has more to say:

I have been waiting for you to come back again. I want to speak to you mother to mother.

After some experiences I had in the past, I didn't want anyone near me, especially not a stallion, or a person with an implement to make me pregnant. The riding ring in that place was a prison, and I am relieved to not ever have to go there again. This you already know.

Everything changed when I came here. After a while I could feel the growth of new desire in my body. I was afraid but also excited on the day the stallion mounted me (Juano). Do under-stand, though, that I have no interest in another pregnancy. Not yet, and not now. My foal Martha, as they named her, was born not too long ago. Most of the time she is right by my side. I am so happy to know this feeling of motherhood again. Yes, I am a mother, and I want to make it right.

You may ask what I mean by "make it right." It's something I am anxious to explain. First, it means that I want to give this foal of mine the care that I never had. But even more than that, I am concerned for the baby's well-being. She needs me right now. She needs all I can give to her. Not just my milk, but my energy too. Something is not quite right. I see how the humans here look at her with worried looks in their eyes. What must be made right is my baby. For me, nothing is as important right now as my child.

I watch the other foals, how they notice so much around them, and I sense how alive they feel. Martha feels quiet on the inside. Her being is slower than theirs. Her eyes have a flatness about them, not sparkling like the eyes of the other young ones here. We must give her more time. I must give her my full attention. I must see that she grows strong enough to have a secure role in this place. I don't want her to be taken away if she is not what they expected. Ask them, may she stay if she is not perfect? And so I make this request: to be given the time to devote to her. Right now it is she who needs my energy, not some new foal-to-be.

They say they have noticed a difference in me, that I seem less interested in the trail rides. Don't worry about that, because I am fine. Please know that for now, it's my baby who has my full focus. I speak to you as a mother. What else can I possibly do?

AMARILLO

It was not easy to fathom, but I'd finally come to accept that if I were going to do this, to truly interpret the speaking of a horse, I would have to trust exactly what I hear during my times of communion with the horses, and would sometimes have to accept as real exactly what I am shown. Such was the case with Amarillo.

Amarillo was no longer being used for trail rides because he wasn't feeling well. He'd stopped eating normally and was losing weight. He'd been having difficulty eating and was cribbing, a compulsive behavior of gnawing and sucking in air. His physical examination revealed nothing unusual. He was getting weaker each day, leaving Debbie and her veterinarian at a loss for what do to.

I asked Amarillo what was going on. He didn't say anything, but he directed my eye to his jaw, showing me an image of something resembling an abscess embedded deep underneath. I described it to Debbie who then told the veterinarian what I'd seen. But still, the veterinarian could not find anything wrong. Two weeks later, an abscess ruptured under his jaw and oozed foul yellow fluid. He had a massive infection in his jawbone and needed a surgical procedure to remove the infected bone. It was a complicated procedure and Amarillo required intensive care for six weeks in order to recover.

PENINA

It was low tourism season, so there were few guests and it was a quiet time at the cabin retreat. Debbie had the time to get away from her office tasks for a while, so we went to visit Juan José at the neighboring farm.

Among the growing number of horses there was Penina, a horse with excellent bloodlines who is now used mostly as a brood mare. At one time she was a very talented dancing horse known for her beautiful gate. She bore many high quality foals, but when her former owner doubted she could conceive again, he decided to give her away. Juan José happily took her in, hoping she would have more foals with his champion stallion, Caretto. When I spoke with Penina, she was 23 years old:

> *They hope that I am pregnant with Caretto's baby. You have great dreams for my foal. I do too, but it's hard for me to relax about being pregnant when there are such high expectations. I feel pressured when you look at me with such hope and excitement for what might be. Please let me know that no matter what happens, I still will have a place with you and you will still see me as me, and not just as a potential mother-to-be. And when a new foal comes to us, let it also be who it will be, no matter who that is. We horses who live here are deeply grateful. We know that this is a paradise. I want my child to live here, too, with me. That way she will always be free.*

I have a bond with Cendri [Juan José's wife] that makes it possible to connect with her while she sleeps. We share much, mother-to-mother, woman-to-woman. I speak to her in her dreams, and she answers me. If there is a pregnancy, it will be important for her to pay close attention to her dreams. She should share them with Juan José and he should trust what she tells him. In this way we can communicate about how the pregnancy is going, and about how I am doing. Remember, I am older now. It takes a lot to carry an unborn horse through to term. I need for Cendri to support me.

Cendri has the ability to hear all of us horses, mostly through her dreams. Now that she has been told this, she will remember more of those dreams.

As it turns out, Penina was pregnant.

CARETTO (2)

Caretto, the horse whose life Juan José had saved, is standing inside a dark stall. I stand outside of the stall and look inside. He looks back at me through the opening between two vertical boards, his dark eyes watching me intently. It isn't long before he speaks:

I remember you. You see now that I am well, that I have become what I knew myself to be.

Our eyes meet.

When you look in my eyes, you can see my strength. In my presence, you feel my power. It is awesome to you, but you are not afraid. Others fear my wildness. You do not; you celebrate it. You see that my spirit is free. I note that you sense my power. You wonder about what I am seeing in you, what I am thinking and what I may have to say.

I want to speak about Juan José. Even before his birth, Juan José knew in his soul who he was meant to be, and he carried that awareness into childhood. But after a while, he began to doubt himself and his identity, because others did not acknowledge him or see

him for who he truly was. As a result, he began to ignore the deepest part of himself, and he weakened inside. The eyes of his spirit closed, and he slept for a while in a state of forgetfulness, believing in what others saw rather than in who he knew himself to be.

There is something I wish for him to understand, but first you must explain to him that our souls can choose where and when to be born into embodied life. Humans have souls. Horses have souls, too. All souls come into life with a purpose to learn and to attain wisdom. Usually this requires the hardship and pain of life experiences, and we often need the help of others in order to grow.

Juan José and I are as one. We have come to this life to help each other. Together we are growing strong. We purposely reunited, and our souls made choices that would allow us each to grow through struggle and hardship, together, into greater wisdom and understanding of ourselves.

This was the agreement our souls made before we were born: that we would help each other to learn that we are who we are, despite what others believe us to be. We must remember and hold strong to ourselves. We agreed to provide each other the help that would allow us to remember who we are at depth.

When I was seen as worthless and sickly in the eyes of others, I became sick in my own mind and then in my body, too. I forgot myself. My eyes closed on my own soul, and I began to die. That suffering made it possible for Juan José and me to find one another. When we met, his eyes opened wide. He knew who I was, and I recognized him as well. The bond we had shared even before birth was still there. His soul memories returned, and he learned to recognize in himself the voice of his own heart.

He knew I was a broken horse, but he saw the real me inside.

When Juan José recognized me for who I really am, it made me want to remember myself. I became angry about my state of being, about what I had allowed to happen to me as a result of my own false beliefs about myself. I stopped accepting the beliefs of others. Juan José changed my name to Flaco because that represented how he was feeling about himself. When he changed it back, it was because I wanted to be seen for who I was. That marked the beginning of my healing and of Juan José's recognition of who he really is.

The sacrifice I made when I chose to come into the world to suffer was not only for the benefit of Juan José, however. My own soul also needed to learn that, unless we are strong enough to remember who we are, we become what others see in us.

If I had not remembered, I would have died.

By rescuing me, Juan José rescued us both. Now Juan José *st awaken fully so that he can fulfill his life's work with horses. y challenges and opportunities will come to him, and he must be strong in his conviction that he truly knows horses: how to train them, ride them, care for them, and be with them. When others doubt his abilities, he must remain clear in his own mind and heart that this is his talent, his work. This is his gift. He must remain a strong leader and trust his own judgment when it involves horses in any way. He must remember, "I am that I am," as I, too, had to remember the same.*

He must now awaken to the truth of his being. He carries inside of him the spirit of the horse. This spirit will never leave him, unless he denies himself.

I was learning about the essence of soul-of-horse as an embodiment or expression of the life force, a particular energetic field out of which each individual horse is formed. Every horse is an individual, with a unique personality, spirit, physiology, and physique. Just as with humans, genetics, environment, and how they are treated and cared for influence horses. Soul-of-horse, the source of each horse's being, exists outside of and prior to the individual physicality or embodiment of the animal. It is this soul-of-horse that I believe is working through and with me during communications.

When Debbie and I pulled into the driveway, back at the cabin retreat, I noticed a horse standing behind the fence along the entrance to the property. "Who is that?" I asked, sensing the horse had been waiting for our return. Debbie replied and I realized what should have been obvious. No other horse is so gorgeous, with her distinctive features and markings, as Beauty.

We decided to go say hello. So we parked, and then walked across the driveway and along side of the stable to where Beauty was standing. I had an odd feeling, as if she was somehow drawing me towards her.

"Hi Beauty!" I said, standing on the other side of the fence.

I wanted to understand what was happening with the horse communication process, and perhaps it was mutual. She seemed to want me to gain a deeper understanding of what she wanted to share.

"Who are you horses, and why is this communication happening between us?" I asked her. "This is all such a mystery to me."

Beauty responded with a simple command:

I will give you the answer to your question. But first go back to your cabin, alone. Put yourself into a receptive state. Take your pen and paper out and listen for me. I will explain to you what needs to be known. You are to write it all down.

"Let's go," I said to Debbie. I thought I'd understood Beauty's request and was intrigued about the prospect of doing as she'd said. Debbie and I walked away and I shared with her what had happened in the exchange. I was anxious to try the exercise Beauty suggested, but suddenly doubted myself and questioned if I'd heard correctly. So I turned and headed back toward Beauty.

"Are you saying that from a distance you'll communicate with me, and give me something to write about that will help me understand all this?"

Beauty turned herself completely around, until it was her rump that was facing me.

"Okay. I've got it," I exclaimed, chuckling. As we continued walking on towards the office, Debbie glanced over her shoulder. "Look, Rosa!" (The name I am called in Costa Rica.) "Look at how Beauty is watching you," she exclaimed. Beauty had turned back around, and was studying me intently as we moved away. From a distance I can hear her say:

Keep going. I am waiting for you.

Twenty minutes later I am settled back in the cabin. Looking out towards Arenal, I say a prayer, offering myself to Divine Will and asking for help in opening to the flow of communication between Beauty and me. I remember my first visit to Costa Rica, and the encounter I had with Arenal. I recall falling to my knees in tears, feeling, hearing, and sensing the living earth. I had offered myself that day in prayer to God to be used as an instrument of Earth's healing and restoration to balance.

I close my eyes and center in. I feel that Beauty is with me. As her words flow, I write them down. When it seems we are finished, I thank her, put the notebook away, and sit for a while longer in a centered prayer of surrender. I sense the "still small voice" move within me. It's not very often I hear that voice, but whenever I have it has made an indelible impression. I am aware that God within me is posing a question about the horses and my capacity to hear them. Am I willing to continue, and to take their messages out into the world? I feel my heart beating more quickly and offer my reply:

"Yes. Thy will be done."

GITANA AND BEAUTY (a farewell)

On the final day of that brief May visit, Debbie and I spent an entire afternoon riding. She took Gitana and I rode Beauty, and the horses' foals and Debbie's two dogs came along. We rode down the unpaved road that runs along the cabin retreat property to a cattle gate opening to the neighbor's farmland. Debbie leaned over carefully to unlatch it, and we climbed up onto the fallow field. After a while we took off in a slow trot up the gradual slope. I felt glorious and alive in the open pastureland, under a huge sky on a bright blue day in May. The grass had grown tall on the rolling hills, so I didn't think the horse could see the ground, but she seemed confident enough to lead the expedition. It hadn't rained much recently, so the ground was dry and easy to navigate on horseback. What a surprise when suddenly, I find myself sliding from the saddle yelling, "I'm falling off!" to Debbie.

Time slows, and I drift to the ground. I land on my back and fear rises in me at the sight of Beauty's front hoof just inches from my head. But she steps aside, not on me, and stands still. I seem to be just fine. Debbie rides over to my side.

"Are you alright?" she asks in her matter-of-fact, unemotional nurse's voice. I mumble something in reply, but I am spellbound by how vast and bright and beautiful the sky appears from where I am lying.

"Can you stand up?" she persists. I hear her, and am sure I can stand, but I don't want to move and I don't feel like talking. It is so peaceful to look up at the white puffs floating overhead against the clear, wide blue, framed by tall yellow grasses all around me.

Time has stopped. The universe is calm, and I feel no urgent need to start the clock again.

"I think you should try to get up," Debbie presses. (Later she shares with me that her major concern was the possibility of poisonous snakes in the tall grass.)

"Come on, Rosa. I think Gitana just said, 'put her on me and I'll take care of her,'" Debbie persists.

Debbie gets down from Gitana. I stand up, aware of having a mild headache yet determined to get right back on the horse. Gitana holds strong as I climb up onto her back. Once in the saddle, I am fully conscious and aware, but inexplicably peaceful.

It was my second fall from a horse. It was a strange fall, without explanation. "I don't know how this happened," I say.

Debbie grins. She wonders if this one is Beauty's doing , that the horse actually intended for me to fall.

We continue on, with Debbie riding Beauty and me now on Gitana. The vistas from up on the high hillside are spectacular. We see the volcano in detail, its grassy patches interspersed with the hardened grey matter from an old lava flow. We stop for a moment to take it all in, and Debbie tells me her story.

When she first visited Costa Rica, Debbie had simply come to vacation. She had no inkling she would one day establish a small retreat and horseback-riding center for tourists. She'd never even ridden a horse. Yet today, horses are central to her business, and many of her guests come primarily because of the opportunity to ride. Debbie visited Costa Rica many times before deciding to move there permanently. She, too, had felt the powerful tug of the Arenal volcano and had given up her job as a neonatal intensive care nurse and moved to Costa Rica with her husband, Steve. Together they created the cabin retreat and a full-scale horse operation based on principles of natural horsemanship.

"Except that you didn't have any experience with horses before!" I affirm.

"Yeah, I know," she says.

Perhaps her desire to move was in response to an inner call from the depths of her soul. Or is it possible that the soul-of-horse, connected to Gaia and Arenal, chose *her* for this particular work, *here*? I sometimes feel that my many trips to be with Debbie and her horses have been a response to a calling from something much larger, something far beyond myself. I certainly never intended to spend so much time in Costa Rica, let alone to talk to horses there.

We continue our afternoon trek over the hillside, across a pasture, along a dirt road and down into the forest below. We walk and sometimes trot past humble, remote homesteads where banana and coconut plants grow tall and see avocado and mango trees green and yellow with ripening fruit. Milk cows stand under nearby sheds while chickens and roosters peck at the packed dirt of their pens. Clothing hangs drying in the open air, and dogs bark as we pass.

I think about the lives of those who live inside these simple homes of corrugated metal roofs, thin concrete walls, and floors that are sometimes no more than packed dirt. How remote these homes are, and how very exposed to the elements of the natural world. What must it be like to live among the people of the country that some researchers have determined to be the happiest in the entire world? As Gitana's strong body moves under me, I think about my own life, about the layer upon layer of protective emotional muscle built up around the tender points of my being.

I remember my first pregnancy, and how after two weeks of joyful fantasies I stood in disbelief over the toilet bowl, staring at its gruesome contents. Something was very wrong. It never occurred to me that I could lose it; I'd never heard of a blighted ovum. The doctor explained it to me just before he vacuumed the remaining contents of the unattached fetus from my womb. We were brave and tried again. The second pregnancy was full term and the fetus' sex had been revealed, so we went ahead and named her Zoe, the Greek word meaning life, and decorated the nursery. At 38 weeks gestation I had a very disturbing dream, which led me to the obstetrician requesting an internal exam. Once again life had deceived me. Two weeks later our first-born daughter was born with the condition of anencephaly, which means she was missing a brain. Her death soon thereafter was inevitable.

So far away in time I am from her.

Zoe was cremated, and we planted a young weeping cherry tree next to her ashes. The tree was blown down in a hurricane, as if she was telling me to let her go. But I continue to keep her spirit with me, inside my heart. When our next child, a son, was ready to be born, I held him inside as long as I could, resisting the opening of the cervix that would allow him to come into the world.

"No," I thought. "It's too dangerous to be born. As long as you are with me, I can protect you." But nature overwhelmed my protective will and eventually pushed him out of my body and into my arms, where I held him tightly to keep him from being snatched away. Yet I know he has never belonged to me, rather to life, with the formidable challenges it brings for him: febrile seizures in infancy, the urgency to treat an entrapped artery throwing clots in adolescence, and the ongoing condition of bi-polar disorder.

In the high country rainforest of Costa Rica, at such distance from my living daughter and son, I struggle over how I can protect them. I sense both held deep inside my gut, in my desire to shield them from life's harsh realities. Sometimes I feel as if I can barely breathe. I wonder if they feel smothered. What would happen if I were to release them into the embrace of life itself?

When we cross a river, Beauty goes directly to the other side, but Gitana stops, smacking her hoof across the water.

"No!" Debbie cries when she sees what the horse is up to. "Keep her going or she'll sit down!" I kick her gently and she continues. We reach the other bank and ride up into the woods.

"Gitana wanted to take a swim," Debbie explains.

"Well, why not?" I ask. "Can't she?"

Debbie hesitates, and then sighs, "Okay."

We turn back down the trail to a small clearing by the riverside. Once we remove the saddles and bridles, Beauty and her foal head straight for the water. Gitana and I wade in, followed by her baby, as Debbie watches from the riverbank.

"Play with her, Rosa!" Debbie shouts, encouraging me.

"But I don't know how!" I call back.

Knowing how to play was a problem for me even when I was a child, and I know from my conversations with Gitana that she is like me in that way. We are two females who have spent the better part of our lives feeling grown up and responsible, never knowing that it is okay sometimes to just play.

Debbie persists. "Splash the water with your hands. See how Beauty is splashing with her leg? Imitate her. That's how they play!"

I look at Gitana, and she looks back at me as if asking my permission to relax and enjoy herself for a while. I splash reluctantly at first, but soon am making bigger and more numerous pounds of my hand against the water. Gitana responds by lifting her leg and slamming it onto the water. Soon she is splashing too, and I am laughing, and then we are both down in the water together, learning to play and experiencing the jubilation that comes with it. My clothes are soaked through to the undergarments, and yet, I can hardly care less.

On the ride back, we come to an incline in the trail, a familiar spot to Beauty and Gitana where they begin to sense they are approaching home. Beauty and Debbie take off running with the two foals following close behind. Gitana lets me know she wants to run too, so I lean forward and let her gallop, my body bouncing to her gait, one hand gripping the reins and the other squeezed tightly around the saddle's horn. As Gitana runs faster, I feel myself releasing the grip of responsibility that doesn't belong to me. Gitana has taken the lead and is protecting and caring for me on this ride. She is the strong one now. All I have to do is hold on and entrust myself to her.

Once at the barn, I dismount and thank Debbie, Gitana, and Beauty for the wonderful ride. It has been a day unlike any other. I am in ecstasy, an awakened state: alert, aware, and alive in a way I've never been before.

VII

EQUINE ENCOUNTERS:
BLUE STAR'S LOVE

I had to leave to catch up with the study-abroad expedition, but to my delight, Debbie joined me on the ship as it sailed from Costa Rica to Peru, Ecuador, and Panama. On board, we had lots of time to talk about what we had learned from and about their horses during my stay. Debbie had come to feel even more strongly that I should write a book on the subject, and I had begun to agree with her. First, though, I needed to ask myself some questions, and hopefully find the answers. Was it just Costa Rica? Did my ability to hear the voices of horses depend on a particular geography, or on my state of mind when living in that culture? I wanted to find out the limits of my capacity to communicate with horses.

Back home in Virginia, I met a woman named Priscilla who boards horses and whose facility is also used as a rest home for retired horses. I shared with her my keen interest in horses, and my newfound clairaudience with regard to them. She'd experienced such a thing before, when a visitor with the same ability spoke to each of her horses and shared with Priscilla what each had to say. Graciously, excitedly, she invited me to visit her farm. I was excited, too, and a week later Bill and I drove out to see her.

There'd been a dusting of snow that morning; enough to delay the opening of county schools, but little remained on the ground by the time we set out under the bright afternoon sun. Our thirty-five minute drive south from the city of Charlottesville took us into Nelson County. Crossing a narrow bridge over the Rockfish River, we quickly found ourselves off of state-maintained paved roads and on an unpaved private lane that wound through dense woods. At the end of the lane, two old stone pillars marked the entry into the property. From there a winding drive took us into a clearing that opened up to wide pastures, and at the top of the drive, expansive vistas of rolling hills and the distant Blue Ridge Mountains lay beyond us. Just beyond a grove of trees and the historic home nestled underneath them, we found the horses, their fields and the barn.

It was a cold winter day. I opened the car door and was greeted immediately by two large, happy Labradors, one black and the other chocolate. I petted them both; feeling entirely welcomed, and stepped out into the brisk air. Priscilla waved to us from just outside of the barn doors. As Bill and I walked in her direction, I realized it was colder than I'd thought. He continued on to the barn while I returned to the car to bundle up a bit more.

I noticed that some of the horses that were out in the field were also heading toward the barn, and a feeling of great joy came over me.

"Pay attention to this feeling," I told myself as my heart leapt. "This feeling reveals something significant." I was about to be with horses again, and my anticipation was mounting.

Grateful and happy to be there, I stepped into the barn where Priscilla and Bill were talking.

What struck me first was how very large the horses were. Unlike the smaller breed that is common in Costa Rica, these were tall, hefty American Quarter Horses. I took a breath and then exhaled my fear, reassuring myself that as long as I remained confidant and calm, no harm would come to me. The size of these horses would not prevent me from making a connection.

My second impression was that all the horses were distracted, and Priscilla explained that it was feeding time. I waited while she scooped food out of the bins and into the buckets, giving each horse their meal. After they ate, I sensed that they were ready to speak with me.

Priscilla and I moved from stall to stall, from horse to horse for the communication. Though the late hour and setting sun allowed for only five conversations that day, I was heartened to discover that the ability to hear and connect was alive in me, and that every horse I met that day had something interesting to say.

Blue Star was the most memorable horse at Priscilla's farm.

We'd spent some time across the center aisle from the place where Blue Star was stabled, as we had been trying to communicate with a palomino named Casper. But Casper was hyperactive and not ready to have a conversation, so I suggested we approach Blue Star. But when we stepped into his stall, Priscilla and I were still talking about Casper and how much smaller he is than the other horses. Because of his relative size, Casper has to work hard to maintain his status in the herd. Blue Star looked down at me, his eyes serious and penetrating:

Why are you in here if you are still focused on Casper over there? Be there if you are still there. If you want to talk with me, then put your attention and focus here with me.

He was right, and I was taken aback. This magnificent, stunning horse was already establishing his ground rules and boundaries. He came over to stand right in front of me, his head towering above mine. As he sniffed my face, I reminded myself to stay calm.

Blue Star is Priscilla's personal horse. They've been together since he was young, and he was raised by her and has lived here all his life. I told Priscilla what he had said as I stood before him, humbled and totally focused.

"I can understand you, Blue Star," I explained. "I have learned to communicate with horses but I am still learning. Maybe you can teach me something that will help me to better use this gift."

You and I don't have a relationship. I don't even know who you are. I thought you were here to help Priscilla. Or is this visit about you? It's Priscilla I care about, which is the only reason I am willing to talk to you.

He'd done it again. And now it was clear whom I was dealing with. Blue Star was regal and self-aware. I asked his permission to touch him and then placed my hand gently on his side.

"He never lets anyone touch him," Priscilla exclaimed as I stroked.

In a whisper, I explained to him my purpose for being there, my willingness to listen, and my capacity to translate. Blue Star noticed how the wind had picked up and was howling across the roof of the barn.

I like to run fast like the wind.

Then he spoke of his devotion to Priscilla, and of how he responds to her slightest movement when she rides him, and reacts to what she is feeling. He also shared his concern:

There is a fear in her. I want to know why, and what it is.

I released my hand and stood back to translate. Blue Star's head lowered toward the ground, and he began licking and chewing.

"He never does that for anyone" Priscilla exclaimed. "I've never seen him lower his head that way."

Priscilla looked at Blue Star and admitted to me that she had lately grown increasingly afraid of being hurt while riding him, aware of her own aging and increasing vulnerability and of Blue Star's tendency to buck.

Why would you be afraid of me? What have I done to cause that? Why would I ever hurt you? After all we have been through, don't you trust me by now?

She spoke of a time, year's back, when Blue Star was young and she fell off of him as a result of his bucking. And she said that she wants to be assured by him that he still understands that she is the alpha in their relationship.

Blue Star lifted his head high and stepped aside.

You really believe that? Look at me, at how much larger I am than you. Look at my powerful physique and the strength of my body.

Priscilla chuckled nervously, replying that she knows that if he wanted to he could buck her off at any time. "But I am still the alpha here!" she reminded him.

How can you look at me, seeing who and what I am, and ever think that you are the alpha? You have been fooling yourself!

"That's exactly the problem," Priscilla said. "Blue Star and I have been struggling over this issue for years."

"It seems you two have a lot more work to do on that aspect of your relationship," I replied. "Neither of you is willing to compromise." Priscilla reached up to place her hands on the face of her beloved horse. And he said:

I will take care of you, Priscilla. You have nothing to fear. I know what you are asking of me and I will try.

"And I will try, too," Priscilla replied.
As we were leaving the stall, Blue Star said to me,

Please tell Priscilla that I love her.

"And I love you too, Blue Star!" she returned.
A week later I received this message:

Rosalyn,

Thank you so much. Your visit to my farm and to the horses in my care was one of the high points in my life and I believe it will always be with me. When I think about the conversations we had, it just brings the tears to my eyes as did your recounting of the conversation with Blue Star—that was a truly memorable experience for me—and nothing he said surprised me in the least. He is an amazing being! I want to share with you that I was so very impressed with your abilities in communicating with the 5 horses. I hope it's okay for me to tell you that I was quite sure that you were not a horse person (i.e. one who has grown up with horses and spent their life in close proximity) but the quality of the individual conversations so exceeded my expectations and your precise understanding of everything each horse had to say was flat out remarkable and I really cannot tell you how extremely fortunate I felt to witness that. I just can't wait for your next visit.

Priscilla

On my next visit to Priscilla's farm, five horse owners who board with Priscilla were there to meet me. With each one I stood in a stall with their horse and interpreted what their horses said. It was a cold day in February, and I'd been so completely engaged with each horse-owner pair that I hardly realized my fingers and toes were nearly frozen. At the end of the visit, Priscilla asked if I might check in with one of her personal horses. He was somber and grieving deeply. He told me that he was also quite angry.

"Why is he angry?" Priscilla asked. She seemed surprised to hear it. But she entirely understood his answer.

I am angry because of the death of my friend. Why wasn't more done to save his life? The veterinarian had to know what was happening, but she never came to help. Is that what will happen to me? Will I, too, soon be left in the field to die? It's not her fault. I suppose it's no one's fault. This is what happens, isn't it? I am angry because I miss my friend terribly, and I feel so lonely here without him, and I don't want to die.

Priscilla's expression was compassionate yet pained. She knew what he was referring to. "It was shocking and sad for us all," she said of the death of the elderly horse. Priscilla boards retired horses, so her farm is a place where some horses will inevitably pass away. This is, of course, a natural occurrence of aging for all living species. But when other resident horses experience such mortal loss, or even worse, actually witness the death of a fellow equine, it can be very difficult and traumatic for them.

VIII

EQUINE ENCOUNTERS: FALLING INTO BLISS

I made arrangements to return to Costa Rica in August, but had to cancel those plans at the last minute due to time constraints in preparing for the coming fall semester. I place the horse book project on hold and turn my attention back to my university teaching. But one day in late November, during my morning meditation and prayers, I again heard the "still small voice" inside of me. The message was clearly leading me back to Costa Rica and urging me to take my daughter Kaya along to photograph the horses. The voice was undeniable; I was going back. And my son Ari was to come with us.

Between Kaya's exams and my classes, we had to schedule the trip for the week after Christmas. We'd focus on photographing each horse I'd previously met and spoken with. I wondered whether there might be other Costa Rican horses I could meet and communicate with while there. I arranged a two-night stay on the far western side of the Arenal volcano, in a bed and breakfast by the lake. Charlie, the host, owns horses and agreed to let me come and visit with them.

"Let's go see if we can find those horses," I tell Kaya on the morning after our arrival at Charlie's place.

Kaya picks up her camera and accompanies me to the pasture behind his home. Four horses stand grazing in the field. We stand too, for nearly thirty minutes, waiting and coaxing, hoping they will respond to my offer to speak with them. But whenever we move a bit closer, they wander further away. All of my other horse communication has taken place in a stable or a barn, but here the horses are free to roam wherever they want. They seem to have no interest in me.

One horse, however, standing high above the pasture under a tree, is watching me. The distance is too far and the terrain too steep for us to climb up to him, so I try to send him a telepathic invitation to come down to where we are. He doesn't seem to respond. I figure that the horse communication must require either captivity or a different method of training. So Kaya and I return to the front porch of Charlie's home to gaze at the view of Arenal.

A few hours later, as Kaya and I are going back into the Charlie's "sky bungalow," I pick up the distinct smell of horses.

"Where are they? Do you smell that?" I ask Kaya as we approach the door to our unit. "I don't see them out in the pasture." I was excited. I'd come here in hopes of hearing other Costa Rican horses. Would I get that chance after all?

We look over the railing of the side porch, and to our surprise, the horse who had been watching us from the hill is standing by the garden gate, as close as he can possibly get to the house. Clearly, he wants to talk. I run for Charlie and ask him to introduce the horse to me. Then I put on my boots to go see him.

"Hello, Ringo. I am Rosa. I have come to meet you. Is there anything you'd like to say? I think I can understand you and promise to send a message back to your owner if you'd like."

Ringo remains very still. I stroke his back. A second horse comes and stands next to him. Then Ringo begins to speak, and I remove my hand from his back and listen. He says,

There was a boy. He lived in the place I used to live. I was very important to him because he was sad and lonely. Whenever he

saw me, he'd come running. When we were together he felt happy and cared for. And he made me feel wanted and needed.

I am clear about what I have heard. Yet deep inside of me are also the words, "There is a girl. She lives in the city of Philadelphia. Aladdin is very important to her because she is sad and lonely. Whenever she sees him she goes running. When they are together she feels happy and cared for. And she makes Aladdin feel wanted and needed."

Ringo continues:

> *But here, I am seen as just another horse, and I don't feel particularly needed. But it's not true. There is someone here, not the one who owns me now, but the one who works for him and cares for us. He is very sad and lonely, just like my friend the boy. He doesn't realize it yet, but he needs me. Tell my owner to let me have time with him alone. Let him ride me, and then he will feel better. And I will feel better too.*

When we are back at his house I look for our host Charlie to let him know what I have heard. He tells me he knows nothing of Ringo's background, having purchased him at an auction. But he is open and willing to listen to me, and seems to take seriously what I have interpreted.

But what had I actually heard? Was it what it appeared, the request of a horse named Ringo to be seen and appreciated for who he was? Or was this horse also telling me about myself, reminding me of the loving presence of Aladdin, which had never left my heart?

Our visit to Charlie's Bed and Breakfast ended with a hike down to the river with Charlie and his family followed by lunch, under a thatched roof hut on the riverbank that had been prepared by his Nicaraguan wife over an open fire. She'd lived alone in the forest during the Sandinista revolution and was familiar with the properties of edible plants. I'd been feeling unwell since we'd arrived in Costa Rica, with a heavy, burning sensation in my lungs that made my breathing labored and tight. She had picked fresh lemon grass and had steeped it in a cauldron of water over the fire. I sip the tea with gratitude and felt much better after drinking it.

When Debbie came to get us, she joined in our outing. We sat on boards, under the canopy of a dense tropical forest, eating freshly made hot tamales and fruit. I wondered what it meant that I was there again, back with the horses in Costa Rica. We finished our meal, said goodbye to our hosts, and hiked back up the trail out of the forest. Then we moved on to the cabin retreat, where for the next few days we devoted ourselves to photographing each of Debbie's horses.

Like a proud mother on school picture day, Debbie had made sure every horse was washed down and neatly brushed for the shoot. I told her not to expect the prettiest photos to be selected for the book. As I explained to each horse, the purpose of our visit was to capture the horse's essence, not just his or her attractiveness or form. I ask the horses to do their best to convey who they feel themselves to be, so that those who read about them can get a clearer sense of who they are. Each of them responds differently to the request, but it is obvious to me that they all understand exactly what I am asking of them.

Beauty is first and is taken into the corral. I remind her of my request, "Let Kaya see who you are on the inside so she can capture your image to share with those who will read about you in the book." She trots once around the ring and then darts straight for Kaya, who is standing just outside the fence. She stops suddenly with her face just shy of the camera. Kaya jumps back, and then Beauty does the same thing again, charging around the ring and then stopping right in front of Kaya. When it is Juano's turn to be photographed, he walks off into the woods with Kaya following behind him, seeking a place where they can be alone. Then he pees, which horses do to mark their territory. As for Caretto, he hears and understands me, then runs and runs across the field until Juan José finally catches him. He stands proudly by his devoted owner for the shot.

On the day before we leave for home, Kaya, Ari, and I all go on a trail ride. Debbie comes along, too, with three other guests and Enrique and Chito, the guides. It has been raining hard almost every night and into the day. Once off the road and on the trail, the horses slip and slid often on the muddy ground. Enrique finds a termite nest, gets down from his horse, and asks if anyone wants to eat one. To my surprise, first Ari and then Kaya answer, "Yes!" and I watch in shock as they each put a termite into their mouths.

We continue on, single file, along the trail. We climb up a steep hill and Gitana, the horse I am riding, gets her front hoofs stuck in the mud. She shifts her weight to prepare to thrust herself forward. From behind me, I hear Debbie yell, "Pull back on the reins!" That command, it turns out, was not intended for me but rather for Ari, whose horse was precariously close behind us. I pull back. Gitana's rear goes down and as it does, I slide off her backside and over her tail, and end up knee deep in the mud. My shoes are sucked in so hard that I can't lift my feet to pull them out. It is my third fall from a horse.

When it is time to go back to the States, I go to the barn to say goodbye. The horses seem disappointed that I haven't asked if they want to talk with me. Unfortunately, I tell them, I wasn't in the proper state of mind to speak with them on this particular trip, since I had to stay focused on the wellbeing of my son and daughter and was also preoccupied with the successful completion of the shoot. I do, however, thank each one for the photos, and let them know I'll be coming back soon. But when I get to Beauty, I pause and ask her if there is anything she wants to share. She stares straight into my eyes and says,

> *We chose you, Rosa. Now put your ego aside and go and do as we've asked you to do. Write it all down as a story. Tell it so that the humans will understand.*

IX

EAT, PRAY, RIDE AND RELEASE

It is true that I'd agreed when Beauty had asked me to listen and share with others what she and the other horses were saying. Writing a book seemed like a reasonable way to do that. But I was not yet ready to begin. I felt empty and unmotivated, lacking the needed inspiration to write.

I'd done my best to make it a merry Christmas for my son and daughter, who had to shuttle back and forth between their dad's house and ours, and Bill and I battled the bumper-to-bumper traffic of Interstate 95 to also spend time with his daughters in D.C. Gifts were opened and meals were shared, and then we returned home. I found myself wondering, what is home? Where is home? Did Bill's children and mine ask those questions the way I still did with each holiday?

I was due to leave again for Costa Rica two short weeks after I'd just come back. It would be my fifth visit in two and a half years. This time I'd be participating in "Eat, Pray and Ride," an eight-day therapeutic "Epona trek." Debbie was bringing me into the leadership team as the resident horse communicator. But I dreaded another plane ride. I was exhausted, and had a college course to plan for spring semester. Furthermore, the thought of another international trip was hard to get very enthusiastic about, especially so soon after my recent visit which had taken place right before the busy holidays.

So I centered myself in prayer and asked, "Why should I go?"

The answer that came to me was quite clear. I needed to see how the group horse therapy process worked, so it could be included in my writing. I resigned myself to going and started to pack. I also arranged to have a session with Hélène, a hypnotherapist who helps people bring awareness to life's turning points.

In the quiet space of Hélène's office, I recline under the warmth of a hand-woven blanket, as the soothing sound of her voice carries me into the deep recesses of my mind.

"Where are you now?" she asks.

"At summer camp," I hear myself reply.

"What do you see? Is anyone there with you?" she continues.

I grimace. She notices. She asks me to describe the scene. We are out in the playing field at the end of yoga class. Everyone has left except the yoga teacher, a male counselor. He and I are sitting in the grass. He is grabbing at my thigh.

"What do you want to do?" Helen asks.

"I want to kick him," I murmur, recognizing my eleven-year-old voice.

"Then do it," she instructs. But I can't. I am not allowed to do such things.

"I want to go to Aladdin," I tell her.

"Not yet," she replies. "Not until you do something about this man."

"I want to go to Aladdin," I whimper. My fingers curl into tight balls.

"Okay. But only if you promise me you will tell Aladdin what happened with that counselor." Aladdin is just on the other side of the fence. I hop over and stand by his side.

"Where are you now?" Helen asks, noticing the softened expression on my face, my relaxed hands, and the greater ease of my breathing.

"With Aladdin."

"Ask him to show you how to kick. Horses are really good at kicking when they need to protect themselves."

In secret, I tell Aladdin how the man had touched me, and how it made me feel really angry. I share with him that I wanted the man to stop, to leave me alone and go away. But I am very confused. I sort of liked how it felt. And I didn't know if the man would get upset with me if I asked him to stop, or if it was safe to complain to him.

"Ask him to show you how to kick, Rosalyn. He can teach you what to do," I hear her say.

"Aladdin, what can I do? I am afraid he'll hurt me if I kick him."

Aladdin instructs me to stand back. Then suddenly he rears back and stands up, his front legs high in the air.

"This is what you do!" he tells me, towering above me, threatening the demise of anyone who would harm me.

"Aladdin is still with you," Helen explains. "He's in your heart. And he's going with you back to Costa Rica."

Just into the New Year, I return to the Arenal cabin retreat. The trip back to Costa Rica takes thirteen hours, beginning with two airplane flights and continuing with a four-hour ride over the mountains from Liberia. Enrique's sister, Lidieth is driving Enrique's airport service van, and her daughter is along for the ride. Lidieth had driven me at least six times before, and between her newly-acquired English and my broken Spanish, we had a great time catching up on what was going on in each of our lives.

That evening, Enrique hosts a barbecue at his home to express his appreciation for the hard work and collegiality of the horsemen, airport drivers, and others who work with him.

Enrique's home is a family compound where his father, sisters, nieces, and nephew live along with him and his wife and children. Located in the center of the tiny town of Monterrey, it serves as a local gathering place for the town. Often, Enrique invites visitors to the lodge to join his family for meals. The barbecue is an informal event held on the back patio of his home, where the large leaves of the coconut trees stretch above our heads.

The sweet and spicy aroma of barbecue wafts in the air along with the smell of marinated chicken cooking on the makeshift grill made from an industrial metal container. The remains of a plate of chicharrón, freshly fried pigskins are all that are left of that dish by the time we arrive. Homemade coleslaw, rice, and stewed yucca, prepared by one of the women, sit in large bowls on a serving table.

Aunts, uncles, cousins, and friends gather to eat and play and drink together. A trampoline occupies the children and teens, while music and chatter fill the cool night air. There is laughter and affection in the air, but also the low murmur of serious gossip. It is a workday, and most of the guests are festive but tired.

I am greeted with hugs and kisses to welcome my return to Costa Rica, and I am introduced to everyone there. Because of the dramatic change in Mr. Big, Erick, a dairy farmer and accomplished horseman, has already heard of me. Intrigue shows in his knowing eyes. "Rosa" is now a familiar name.

I meet Erick again in the morning at Debbie and Steve's cabin retreat. He is in the stables preparing to guide a trail ride. Erick had been raised on a farm and taught by his father from a young age how to work with horses. The horses respect him and do exactly as he directs. His booming voice, with its strong tone of command, gets an immediate response from them. He carries himself with impressive authority. But Dorado is the exception.

According to Erick, Dorado turns his face away and tries to buck him off if Erick attempts to ride him. Dorado's will is strong, and he is tenacious in his disregard for Erick. I understand that Erick and Dorado have some history together on the rodeo circuit. Erick asks Debbie in Spanish if I would be willing to speak with Dorado, whom he felt was uncongenial to him. He and I approach Dorado together. The horse is eating hay from the concrete trough. Dorado shows no interest in talking, despite my persistence in asking, "Please, Dorado, Erick wants to understand why you don't like him. Erick wants to be your friend."

Erick stands patiently as I plead with Dorado to tell me what the problem is. At first, I think Dorado is telling me that there is someone else, a man, who reminds Dorado of Erick, so that Dorado's dislike of Erick was not personal but instead based on his resemblance to someone else. But the more I speak to Dorado, the more I know I am wrong. He isn't saying that at all. In the absence of any reply to my inquiry, I am filling the empty space with conjecture.

I move from behind the fence and make my way over to the other side where Dorado is standing. I lay my arm on his back while he continues to eat and to ignore Erick.

"Look at him standing there," I say to Dorado. "All he wants is to understand why you are so mean to him. Just look in his eyes. Can't you see that he is sad about your relationship with him? Why won't you tell us what's the matter? He

just wants to be your friend."

At that point, Debbie joins us. My Spanish is not fluent, so I ask Debbie to ask Erick if he had ever done anything that might make Dorado angry. Erick nods, acknowledging his occasional heavy-handedness with him, but says he doubts that is the problem. He thinks he treats Dorado reasonably, just as he would any other horse that resists his directions. Dorado has no reason to be angry, he says.

With that the flow of communication begins between Dorado and me:

Tell him to look at himself. He knows what the problem is.
He knows exactly why I don't want to be around him.

Erick is surprised.

"Yo!?" he questions ("Me?"), his eyes wide and eyebrows high. When he begins speaking rapidly in Spanish, I begin to find it hard to listen to Dorado while also trying to understand Erick. I ask Enrique to join us.

"Yes, you," Enrique says, translating my English to Spanish as I continued to interpret for Erick what Dorado was saying.

Think about how you treat me when you see me. Why would
I want to be your friend? You say that's what you want, but you
act like you want to control me, to force me to do what you want
without any consideration for what I might want.

Erick is at a loss. A good horseman is in total control over his animal, of course. How else would he treat him?

Your will is strong. You are strong. I do respect you for
that. But we have no basis for friendship. Why should I want to
be manhandled by you? I don't like that. I have a will, too, you
know. I am powerful, just like you. If you approach me, wanting
to demonstrate your power, what do you expect from me? Adora-
tion? Friendship? Think again. Man to man, my response will be
to show you who is the stronger of us.

Erick's face drops. His expression grows serious and somber. "Then how can we be friends?" he asks.

I told you that I respect you. You have yet to tell me the same.

"What am I to do?" Erick asks. "*¿Qué voy a hacer?*" These words I understand.

"Open your heart to him," I reply. "*Abra su corazón.*"

Debbie comes into the stall to stand by Dorado and me. "Let him know how you really feel," she suggests.

The two of us stand by Dorado. Erick remains on the other side of the wall.

"Come on Dorado," Erick says. "You know I care about you. Why can't you and I be friends?"

Debbie tells Erick that this would be a good time to approach Dorado differently and to openly express his affection and respect for the horse. So Erick climbs over the barrier separating him from Dorado and joins us. He and Dorado are eye-to-eye with the horse.

"Let's be friends," Erick repeats, stroking Dorado on his neck.

Dorado turns around completely, until his rear end is facing Erick, and then he poops right in front of him. Erick jumps back, throwing up his hands and yelling.

"Now can you see what I mean? This horse just doesn't like me!"

"Try again, Erick," I say. "He is only reacting to your pride. Maybe if you put that aside and genuinely reach out to him, Dorado will sense how you truly feel."

Erick's face softens. The look in his eyes, which before seemed to express his determination not to be rejected, changes. Debbie and I looked at one another. We both feel a shift occurring between Erick and Dorado, and see that Erick's heart is opening. He places his arm over Dorado's back, gently stroking his side. Rubbing and patting his back and butt with affection, Erick speaks to Dorado of his respect and admiration and expresses his desire that they be friends, sharing his honest frustration over the long-standing tension and strain that has existed between them.

Dorado lifts his head and turns his neck around to look back at Erick. Something in Dorado has shifted, and he seems to be opening up to Erick for the first time. I know it is just the beginning, that real progress will take time and a genuine and consistent effort on both their parts.

The Epona Trek is scheduled for Wednesday. It is now Monday evening, so participants will be arriving in two days, and we focus our attention on selecting the horses. Debbie and I go into the stable to decide which horse will be assigned to which participant. The Epona Trek leaders, Nancy and Shelly, have already claimed their horses.

Some of the horses seem anxious and excited in anticipation of the eight-day trek. They sense it will happen soon, but they want to know which horses will get to go? Mr. Big and Titán and Beauty are sure picks, but we pass over Amarillo. This is the horse I'd spoken with during my previous visit, the one who'd been cribbing and had shown me an abscess under his right jaw. Amarillo catches my attention and asks:

What about me? Can I go too?

Amarillo had been through surgery on his jaw and is healing well. Debbie feels he needs more time to rest and regain his strength and his appetite before taking on such a big job, and Ronald the stableman agrees with her. But Amarillo does not! He is ready to get back to work.

But I am ready. If you will just take me, then you'll see. I'll be fine.

Debbie will not concede. He is very disappointed.

Debbie notes that Mr. Big has been following me around. He seems very excited to see me again. Everywhere we go in the stable, he is either right behind me or by my side. I am flattered to have his affection, and Debbie gushes with pride and joy over how well he's been doing since I had first spoken with him. Mr. Big was indeed a changed horse, and was now genuinely happy, helpful, and eager to please. Debbie greets him with praise and gratitude, affectionately stroking his mane and saying, "What a good boy you are, Mr. Big!"

I sit on the ledge of the narrow aisle near the place where J.R. is standing. Debbie has asked me to find out if he wants to come along. I settle into a meditative state, centering myself in preparation for the communication. But as I open my eyes, my attention is deflected from J.R. to the horse on the other side of the aisle. He is not looking my way, but I can feel him asking to be heard.

It is still difficult for me to tell one horse from another, so I am not sure who this horse is. Debbie has stepped into the tack room, so I wait until she returns to ask her his name. She tells me he is Conan, the horse who once spoke to me about sensing intentions, the one who called horses the "great communicators" and was surprised that I could understand what he was saying.

I hop down from the ledge and walk over to stand by his side. He feels heavy and sad to me.

"What's the matter, Conan?" I ask. "You look so tired. Are you not feeling well?" It is a while before he says anything:

> *I am tired, yes, tired of being a horse in this world. This is not my first time, you know, coming into the body of a horse to be with humans. It's my third time, and every time it's the same problem. All I ever want to do is to help, but I don't seem to know how. I don't feel like I am making a difference for humans at all. I give up. This is my last time. I am definitely not coming back again.*

He is sullen, down in the dumps, feeling sorry for himself. Just then Mr. Big shows up, because he has something to say, too! He is really joyful, full of life and purpose, and he knows that he is making a difference in the life of every visiting tourist who rides on his back. But he understands that Conan does not feel that way, and he is worried that his own newfound lease on life, and the admiration he is recently receiving, is making Conan feel bad about himself. Conan continues:

> *Look at how excited Debbie is about Mr. Big. She thinks he is just great. Not me, though. When she talks to him, I can hear the enthusiasm in her voice. She never speaks to me that way. Maybe I am just not cut out for this.*

Mr. Big chimes in:

> *I wish he wouldn't feel that way. What I am and how she treats me has nothing to do with him.*

Debbie comes in and notices me with the two horses. "What's going on here?" she asks.

"It's a three-way conversation!" I exclaim. Debbie is saddened by what I tell her about Conan's state of mind.

"He's just like Eeeyore from Winnie the Pooh," she complains, chuckling as she strokes his mane.

I wish she would not make light of this.

Debbie's husband Steve comes into the stable. Sitting on the ledge, he watches and listens. When I tell him what Conan is feeling, he remarks, "But he's just a horse!"

I forgive him for saying that. He just doesn't understand.

Debbie tries to console him by telling him that he is a valued member of the retreat community. She reminds him of a recent rider, a young woman with a substance abuse problem, whose experience with him was affirming and supportive. She was grateful for her ride on Conan, and emotional about leaving him when her stay ended. I continue to try to build up his confidence, but it is not enough. Conan continues to point out to me how obvious it is to him that Debbie doesn't hold him in very high regard, and that she doesn't value his presence or his work. Debbie responds to that with genuine regret, but makes it clear she believes Conan is himself responsible.

"The way you are, Conan, just isn't that much fun for our riders. You don't come across as truly wanting to be with people."

Mr. Big stands by listening.

"You have to at least let riders think they are in control," she continues as she strokes his head. "You have to give them the impression that you are responding to their commands and their directions. If you don't play along that way, they won't feel good about being with you. Who wants a horse that doesn't seem to like them, and won't even listen to them?"

Mr. Big walks away. Conan moves over to the hay bin and begins eating. He is still listening, I sense, but he needs time to consider what Debbie had said to him. Later, away from his presence, Debbie admits, "No one ever picks Conan to ride."

The "Eat-Pray-Ride Trek" is a collaborative effort between Debbie, Shelley, and Nancy of the Epona Center. Shelley and Nancy are Eponaquest Advanced Instructors from the Epona Center in Arizona. On Tuesday we begin to finalize the plans for the trek. We go into the stable to talk about the horses that will be used for the trek and which horse I will ride. Since I have a history of falling off horses, my choice of horse must be considered carefully, as it is not an easy ride. Conan is one of the horses we visit.

I explain to Shelly what Conan had said about doubting his capacity to be successful helping humans. Shelly is surprised, and immediately shares the tale of the same woman Debbie had mentioned before, a rider who had participated in the trek a few months before. That woman felt that being with Conan had changed her life, and asked Shelly to give Conan a kiss for her. She loved and deeply missed Conan. I try to boost his confidence by telling him how valuable he is and how much of a difference he had made to at least one person. I tell him that he should try to believe in himself, because he is needed and important in the therapeutic work. He hears me, and replies:

> *I know all about the young woman who was here the last time. You tell me I made a big difference in her life. You keep telling me how I am needed, and that I should not feel so down about myself. You stand around me speaking about how I need more confidence, and to learn to make riders feel good so they will want to be with me. It all sounds so disingenuous. I know about the trek and that you are in the process of selecting the horse you will ride. If, as you insist, I am so important and so valuable as a therapeutic horse, then why have you not chosen me?*

I am speechless. He is exactly right. I haven't even considered riding Conan, in part because, like others, I do not find him particularly attractive or fun to be around. There are much more beautiful horses in the barn, like my friends Gitana and Titán. Also, Conan seemed to have lost his confidence, and I want a horse that is clear and strong. Conan persists:

> *Take another look at me. What are you actually seeing?*

I look at Conan and see myself looking back at me; me, the one who has lost her confidence and is no longer sure of her own capabilities. The process has begun. The horse that I most need is choosing me. Who was the unattractive one here, Conan or I?

Horses, in their capacity to heal, become a mirror of our inner life. This is where and how the work begins. The horse that chooses us reflects our deepest self to us.

Debbie, Shelly, and I discuss what had happened between Conan and me. We'd originally intended to decide in advance which horses would be put with which rider for the trek, but based on my encounter with Conan, we alter that plan. We decide to blindfold the participants, walk them into the barn, and then let the horses to do the choosing. The inherent human bias of sight, our dominant sense, would be removed. Once selected, the participants might be more likely to perceive the horse through their other senses. It would no longer be a beauty contest.

Wednesday afternoon came, and all the participants gather in a circle on straw bales in the stable. Everyone is introduced and then asked to cover their eyes with a bandana. I read aloud a poem about allowing the horses to teach us. Then we walk blindfolded to the barn and form another circle, this time with the participants standing back to back.

One by one, the horses are brought into the barn. Debbie, Shelly, and I stand back and observe, watching for an indication of which rider is being chosen. In almost every case the selection is clearly apparent, with the horse walking up to the circle and standing in front of a particular person. But when Beauty comes in, she refuses to go near the circle of blindfolded trekkers. She walks right past the group and stands off to the side. When I ask her why, she replies:

> *I want to go on the trek, but I don't want to be ridden by any of these people. My only purpose in going would be to keep an eye on you, Rosa.*

I had already committed to Conan, so Chito would be riding Beauty.

With Gitana it is the same; she is hesitant to pick anyone. Shelley and Debbie encourage Gitana to make a choice. Gitana becomes more and more agitated, to the point of almost kicking Shelley. She stays near Debbie. It is obvious she has chosen her.

After the horses make their selections, I go to each rider-horse pair and share what the horse wants their rider to know. In some cases, the bonding process has already gone so deep that my communication is not needed, but I still share what I hear with each pair. Pica, for example, says:

> *She is holding onto a deep sadness. Tell her it's safe to let it out, to release it. I can handle what she feels. I can carry her and also her sadness. She can cry with me.*

The rider's eyes opened wide, and her tears begin to flow. "How could you possibly know this?" she asks me.

"It isn't me," I explain. "It's Pica. Your horse knows what's going on with you."

Indeed, each horse has chosen just the right person based on their ability to help that particular rider.

There is a lot of activity the next morning in preparation for a full day's ride. All the horses are washed and saddled up, and the trek participants gather the supplies they will pack into the saddlebags. I'd had a terrible night with only four hours of sleep, so I went to tell Conan what I needed.

"Conan, I am exhausted. I can hardly stand up, let alone think. I need for you to take the lead, to make the decisions and use your best judgment so I can close my eyes and rest, even be half asleep, while we are riding."

Conan, who was tied up in preparation for re-shodding, listened to me as I spoke. I believe he understood.

"Please, do the work of both of us. Decide where to step and how, when to move, and when to stop. I am asking you to take full control," I said.

What in the world was I thinking? I cannot ride across these steep hills and valleys.

We all climbed onto our designated horses. Our leaders gave us very specific directions to never let our horse eat while we were in the saddle. Conan began eating from the hay filled trough before we'd even left the barn, and even bit the foals that tried to get the same food.

Our first hour on the trail, Conan grabbed a clump of grass whenever we stopped, and at frequent intervals even when we were on the move. I was unable to control him. Enrique made a joke about it and said that every time a horse ate, its rider would owe him five dollars. It rapidly became a very expensive ride for me. At the end of the second hour on the trail, Debbie suggested that, rather than trying to fight Conan by yanking and pulling at the reigns when he ate, I could try wrapping the reigns around the horn to keep him from lowering his head to the ground. But Conan was faster than I, and the moment we came to a halt he would grab a mouthful of grass before I had time to tighten the reigns. We struggled and fought, and he kept winning. My fine crept up to forty dollars!

About three hours into the trek, miles from our origin, we had crossed two rivers, gone through a patch of rainforest, and were walking through a wide rolling pasture. Up ahead was a huge tree, a Ceiba, which must have been over two hundred years old. We rode up to the base of the tree and Enrique hopped off of his horse with a gleeful shout.

"He's there!" he cried out, referring to a sloth.

He reached towards the tree trunk and scooped up a full-grown animal, cradling it in his arms. I would have enjoyed holding him, as others did. Those who held him exclaimed over how soft he was, and how cuddly, although one woman said his claws were sharp and cut her. But I was too busy to play with the sloth, focused as I was on trying to get Conan to stop eating. His strategy was to keep walking, away from the others, and pull his head down hard so I could not get the reigns wrapped up. I decided to have a chat with him.

"Why are you doing this, Conan? You know I am not supposed to be letting you eat. It's a rule." His reply:

"You are not my boss."

He had a valid point. So I turned around and yelled a question to Debbie. Was there some reason I could give Conan, something to justify the rule, that might convince him to obey my request that he not eat?

"The reason why we don't let them eat," she threw back, "is to establish control so the horse knows who is in charge." Oh. I see. I am supposed to be the boss, not Conan.

"He never does that when I ride him," Debbie continued.

"No?" I replied. "And why do you think that is?" I persisted, thinking I would come out as the capable horse communicator. Debbie grinned.

"Because I don't let him. When I ride him, I am the boss, and I am in control."

I took that as a challenge. Then I remembered: I had asked him to be the boss. I had told him I didn't have the energy to do it. I had given over my authority and control, and now it was up to me to take it back. How often had I done the very same thing in my life? With how many bosses had I given up when faced with a struggle for control? The more I thought about it, the more situations I could think of, even back to my childhood, where I had felt so incapable and weak that I relinquished control to someone I thought much stronger, even when it meant subjugating my own desires and needs. Here was a chance to take back control, to re-establish my authority. I didn't feel tired anymore. In fact, I felt exhilarated.

"Change of plans, Conan," I told him. "Never mind what I said earlier. You will do as I say."

I don't think I'd ever felt so clear and capable before in my life. It took a while for him to believe that I meant what I said, perhaps because I didn't quite believe it myself at first. Here I was, sitting on a thousand-pound animal that would eat all day long if allowed to do so, an animal with the strength and power to toss me off its back and run away even though his training and personality make it more likely he will simply ignore me. But he didn't do any of those things. Instead, the clearer and more self-confident I got, the less he attempted to eat.

We reached the wooded path leading to the waterfall and I dismounted. I was happy to release the reins so that Conan could eat freely. But once I was off his back, he lost interest in the grass at his feet. It was just grass, after all. Apparently his eating had little to do with hunger. Something else was going on.

The trek participants all seemed to enjoy themselves at the waterfall. Most of us took off our outerwear, changed into suits, and swam. Some jumped from a large boulder into the pool below. I thought I saw a snake in a tree, which turned out to be a vine. But the illusion gave me the opportunity to play a trick on Enrique's teenage son, who fell for it when I yelled, "Snake!" In spite of speaking different languages, and across a fairly significant age, gender, and culture gap, he and I enjoyed a wonderful laugh over that. There are many, many poisonous snakes in Costa Rica. Seeing one close by is taken very seriously. Generally, a snake seen is a snake killed.

By the time day one of our trek came to an end, Conan and I had become a productive riding team. He held his head upright and focused on the ride, and he no longer grabbed at leaves and grass. And when he ran, breaking into a gallop, I held on with trust and pride. On the ride back I reflected on the things I thought I had learned that day about horses and about life. First, the more control one has over the horse (and life situations in general), the better the results. Second, the less control one exerts, the greater weakness one has in the eyes of the horse, and other humans. Only later would I come to see that I had much more to learn from Conan, and that these two understandings were incorrect.

Our first day out is almost over. Enrique points up at the sky. I feel a surge of "Ah!' as I catch sight of the white hawk, its broad wings and white body sailing silently across the sky. A long snake hangs from its beak.

"That's my animal totem!" I exclaim to no one, because no one is listening. None of the other riders even look up to see the bird. But these words need not be heard by anyone else. Hawk, the messenger, signifies the awareness and fulfillment of my soul's purpose, and holds the key to awakening to higher levels of consciousness and inspiring life's creative purpose.

Day two takes us to Erick's home, where he has built a facility for visitors. He and his family were our hosts for the evening and provided welcome snacks, dinner, and breakfast the next day. Day three was spent on Erick's farm, where we swam with our horses. Erick has a pond that was originally constructed for tilapia. He, Enrique, and Chito, our guides, took our horses three by three into the water. Once the horses were acclimated, the trek participants were invited to come in. Some of the horses refused to go, and others went in briefly only to jump right back out again. Conan, on whom I was riding, eventually went in after some coaxing from me. But after one lap around the pond with me on his back, he indicated an intention to jump out. Debbie shouted, "Get off now!" to protect me from getting hurt, so I slid off his back into the water. He climbed out. I was grateful to him for trying the pond, however briefly.

It was Juano who most enjoyed the water and who stayed in nearly all afternoon. I waited my turn and then, with considerable help, climbed onto his bare back and grabbed hold of his mane. Sitting up was nearly impossible, so I laid myself down along his back. I could feel his powerful musculature and his strength as he paddled us along. Who was in control this time? Certainly not I. It was all I could do just to stay on.

That night I had a dream. In it, Debbie and I were standing in the dark outside of a very large house. Heavy wooden beams enclosed the great vaulted spaces of the massive dwelling. I could see flames inside, and told Debbie we must go in to make sure no one was trapped inside. We searched all the rooms, and I was especially frantic to find my children if they were in there. But we found no one in the house. The flames were growing taller and the fire was spreading more quickly. I shouted to Debbie, "We have to get out NOW!" and headed down the staircase and out the door. I thought I should go back for a pair of shoes to wear, so I grabbed the footwear and whatever else I could gather and headed out the door just as the flames engulfed the house.

When I awoke in the morning I realized that my own transformation was imminent.

On the third day of the trek, we leave early in the morning from Erick's farm. I pack my saddlebag with necessary provisions I'd brought from my cabin at the retreat: sunglasses, my notebook and pen, a bottle of water, and a snack bar. But I've neglected to bring any sunscreen. And what's worse, I can't find the slow release antihistamine pill I thought I'd stuffed into my pocket. I am afraid I might have a bad allergic reaction to the grass pollens I'd be exposed to. I dig around in all of my belongings and in my five cargo-pant pockets, but without success.

"Darn it," I mumble under my breath. "What happened to that pill?" wondering if I at least have brought along the inhaler my doctor prescribed in the event of an asthmatic response, which I have experienced only rarely, in unusual seasonal conditions. I hope for the best and climb onto Conan's back.

The trek takes us near Arenal, across the mountainous northern region of Costa Rica. Much of the day is relaxing and uneventful. We ride along gravel roads through small towns, passing the church, the school, the solo store, and twenty or so homes of each tiny community. We chat and laugh and are sometimes just quiet as we cross cattle farms and ride through tall grasses, over gently rolling terrain and up the verdant hillsides. Sometimes Enrique notices something worth stopping to see, such as howler monkeys sleeping in trees, or a Guanacaste, the striking, umbrella-like national tree of Costa Rica. A local farmer invites us to stop at his home for a drink of fresh-pressed sugar cane juice. We watch as he pushes the long green stalks into a hand cranked press, the clear liquid running over its spout and into a pitcher from which he serves the refreshing drink.

At another homestead, we stop for an extended visit. Walking through the muddy paths past pigs and chickens and into their home, we find ourselves graciously welcomed. Inside is a long room with a large table covered with a bright green cloth and decorated with fresh flowers. We are seated and served, by the farmer's wife, children, and mother, a full, typical Tico lunch prepared over a wood-fueled stove. The meal is filling and delicious, especially the stewed black beans, fresh fruits, and juices.

As our meal comes to an end, I stand and approach Enrique who is sitting at the far end of the table, talking and laughing with our host.

"Hey Rosa! *Como esta?*" he says waving at me.

"*Bien*," I reply, followed by a confession about being nervous about the rest of our day's trek. "I really hope I don't fall off Conan on our ride down into the valley." Enrique tells me not to worry, and that I will be just fine. (Only later did he confess to me that he was quite concerned about that.)

We thank our host family and gather up the horses in preparation for the most difficult part of the entire trek. Once back up on Conan and out of doors again, I feel the burn from the harsh rays of the sun that had penetrated the skin of my upper back and neck. Forgetting the sun protection was a big mistake. I've eaten too much and want to rest, even to nap perhaps, but to be safe it's important that I stay alert. From here on, the terrain will be much more treacherous than any we have crossed thus far.

As we proceed, I am aware that we are ascending to the height of the ridges that lead down into the Venado Valley. My fears begin to build in anticipation. I've seen the other side of these green gumdrop hills from the farms far below. I know how precipitous a drop awaits us on the other side.

Finally we arrive at the edge of the ridge. I look down. Off to the right, a steep slope leads to a boldly flowing stream. To the left is a dramatic, seemingly endless drop. In between is the narrow cow path we are walking.

I panic. This feels dangerous to me. What if Conan trips and stumbles? I'll fall to my death or be severely hurt, and we are far, far from any emergency care.

I consider the possibility of turning back. I think of getting down and walking, but I am not wearing proper footwear for such a trek, and it would be well after dark before I arrive at the bottom if I try to make it on foot. Besides, some of the trail is too rugged for hiking, and is only accessible on horseback.

For two days I've been riding on Conan's back, negotiating for control with this thousand-pound animal. I've led him where I want him to go and gotten him to start and stop, but still I have hardly any sense of how to handle him well. And now here we are at the height of the trail, and at the height of my terror about our descent. How will I get down this mountainside alive and well?

My stomach tightens. I feel panic coming on. I try to inhale deeply, but my breathing remains shallow, and my heart rate begins to increase. I feel I have never been in a more risky and vulnerable situation.

If I don't return to my home in the U.S., what will happen to my son? I won't be there to care for him if his mental condition grows worse. And how will my daughter manage with me gone? Bill will be very sad and alone, but he'll eventually be okay. My elderly parents still need my support; how horrible it would be for them if I were never to return.

I don't want to die. Not here. Not now. Not in this way. I have no choice but to trust Conan, to relinquish some control to him.

"I'm scared, Conan," I confess to my horse.

Conan replies that he knows very well how afraid I feel, and it is making him anxious and worried. I looked back at our three experienced guides, Enrique, Ronald, and Chito, feeling a glimmer of hope that in their capable hands I have little to fear.

Why are you looking to those men? What can they possibly do? It's my back you are on, not theirs. It's me you need to rely on.

He'd read my mind. And scolded me.

Once again I look down into the valley. What if I fall? What if I fall? What if I fall?

Is this fear really about riding down on Conan? Yes, for this moment in time it is. Absolutely.

"Conan, please do your best to take care of me," I ask. "Go where you need to go. You decide which way is best." Conan continues to speak to me:

First of all, I know what I am doing. Second of all, just stop looking down. And third, keep your focus on me. Look only between my ears at the back of my head.

I take in a deep breath and stare at the space between his ears. Enrique, riding just behind, is clearly aware of my state of anxiety. He reminds me to lean way back in the saddle as we go down. Steadily, Conan navigates the steep grassy slopes, crisscrossing cow paths and narrow ridges into the Venado Valley below. I hold my gaze as he has instructed me, and when I look away at all, it is to gaze up at the sky.

For two and a half grueling hours, we ride down toward the bottomland. Periodically, I remind myself to hold on tightly, and reassure myself that I will be okay. When I feel the fear building up again, I remember what Conan has directed me to do, and I regain my focus on him, trusting that in this way he can take care of me and I will stay on, not fall, and be safe.

But what if it's Conan who falls, with me on his back? He'll crush me under his weight and I will never survive that. My grip on the saddle horn tightens. My body stiffens and my stomach pulls up into a knot.

I can't do this. I don't know how. I have no control whatsoever over this dangerous situation.

But Conan's gait seems steady. His feet seem sure. What if I refrain from anticipating what may happen, of imagining the worst possible outcomes? Perhaps then I will notice something beautiful, even enjoy a few moments of the ride down.

The valley stretches out in front of us in shades of green as far as my eyes can see. Mountain ranges, scattered trees, and forests can be seen in the distance. The sky, wide and bright with late day sun, feels like an opening into the unknown vastness of the rest of the universe. The land beneath feels like home.

I recall when my son Ari was seventeen years of age. (I feel Conan's movements against my calves.) He'd sent me a string of text messages, none of which made any sense. (I gaze across the landscape to the hilly horizon.) His father and I jumped in the car and rushed to the high school Ari attended, trusting that we would find him there. I knew his familiar face as he was coming towards me in the corridor, but did not recognize the look in his eyes. What had happened to our son? "What's going on, Ari?" I asked him. He spoke rapidly, nonsensically about leaving for New York, and how he was on his way there.

In the hospital emergency room they asked him simple questions, like what day and year it was. His answers were bizarre. He was clearly disoriented. So they gave him a diagnosis, assigned him a bed, stripped him of his street clothes, and locked him behind the double steel doors of our collective shadow; the psychiatric ward was where he would be safest, they said. I think it also served to keep him away from those who fear the unpredictability of life, and the potential loss of control. With heavy doses of antipsychotics and tranquilizers they tried to bring him back into a shared reality. But that would be a long time in coming. I looked at my son, and he looked back at me, with fiery wild eyes. "It's time for you to move out of your head," he said, "and start living from your heart." He, the one deemed to be ill, had astutely perceived the sickness in me, about which I'd not even the faintest hint. My son had lost his mind. And I was stuck in mine.

Conan asks if I am okay. I thank him and tell him I am fine. Soon we come in sight of the river. We are almost there. I am elated with anticipation. Navigating the last of the steep slopes down to the river, the path splits into two. Everyone else takes the higher path, but Conan veers off to the lower one.

"Rosa! Not that way, this way!" Debbie yells. But it is too late; there is no way to turn around.

"Conan," I say, "you made this choice. You know what you are doing. And I believe you are taking care of me." As it turns out, the lower path has the best footing and is the safer choice.

We are the first to reach the river. Together, we have made it down safely. "Thank you, Conan. Thank you!" Tears flow, turning into sobs of relief.

Conan stands still by the side of the river as the others come down from the mountainside. Something wells up inside me, yearning to be set free, and an intense pressure moves through my body. The pressure is surfacing. I feel

Conan sigh and relax under me. Finally, I exhale. The blame
I placed on myself for my daughter Zoe's deformity, for the
fact that she was born without a brain, is gone. I let go of
the guilt for taking so many B vitamins during the pregnancy,
which now are known to be toxic to the developing fetus. I
had done what I thought was best at the time; it was not my
fault. Breathing in the sweet mountain air, which feels so very
light, is now almost effortless. I release the responsibility for
her death. With another exhalation, I let go of the belief that
my son's bi-polar disorder may have been prevented if only, if
only, if only I had done this, or not done that, or tried something different, or been someone else. I inhale the fresh air,
embracing the belief that I will find a way to love and be there
for him and to support him whatever his state of mind might
be. As the out breath leaves my nostrils, I expel the guilt and
sorrow I feel over his condition.

Fresh air rises from the aerated water that tumbles along
the riverbed below, filling my lungs with restorative energy.
More tears fall and I exhale again, letting go of my marriage,
saying goodbye to the self that had for so long been defined by
who my husband was, and by the place that together we created as home. In gratitude I honor a wonderful, kind-hearted
man, and our thirty-plus years of love and companionship I
feel free, finally able to redefine what it means to be me.

After a moment, I grow quiet inside. What am I feeling?
Is this my heart that's opening? My breath is light, effortless. My body feels almost weightless. A sense of peace rises
into joy. My mind clear and still, as I unite with the spirit of
Conan.

After the first day's ride on the trek, with Conan battling
me over eating grass, I thought I'd learned that the greater

the control I maintain over the horse (and perhaps over life situations in general), the better the results. And that the less control and clarity I exert, the weaker I am in the eyes of the horse, and other humans as well. I was wrong on both counts. The truth is that relationships, whether with horses or with people, are about sharing control. But it's clarity that makes that possible, knowing what I expect and what I want and also what I need.

I have accomplished an amazing feat, working through and past a deep, gripping fear. Conan has taken care of me. Conan has taught me that if I can remain focused in the present moment, then I can handle even the challenges I fear are insurmountable.

With a greater awareness of myself, and the horse as my trusted companion, I see that strength doesn't come from the capacity to control the horse, or to control the outcome of a given situation. It comes from an inner awareness of one's self situated in one's own inner power, which need not be outwardly displayed. And within the loving process of give and take and the reciprocal exchange of power, fear turns to trust and good outcomes become more likely. I learned that the fear that I thought served to warn and protect me has really only limited and skewed my ability to be wholly present in the moment.

"Great job, Rosa!" Enrique calls to me as he rides past, over the riverbank. "Come this way," he instructs.

Conan steps carefully over the wet boulders and loose rocks, making his way across the river. I feel fear, but it quickly dissipates. Conan is carrying me. I have entrusted him with this responsibility. I release the tension in my muscles and let Conan work on my behalf, and do the job I cannot do.

If I had gained any wisdom as a result of the descent into Venado Valley, it was that I needed to let Conan take care of me. And that is exactly what he wanted to do. While it may be true that humans have a huge influence on Earth and her creatures, we remain mere co-inhabitants, equal but not superior to other creatures. We are not more significant than they. Our spiritual awakening depends on recognizing that we are co-evolving with our fellow creatures, as interdependent earthlings with them. I succeeded in the ride down the mountainside because I found my strength and the courage to ride, but I would never have made it if not for Conan's love and his commitment to me.

How will I mark the occasion of such a rebirth as this? What needs to be done to symbolize this release, and the movement into a new way of being?

When we arrive at our final destination farm, I dismount, pat Conan, and take the helmet off my head. My hand goes spontaneously to my hair. I feel its thickness, seven years' worth of growth, and pull my fingers through from scalp to ends where the twisted strands hang just above my shoulders. The natural gray roots dominate the tinted ends of golden brown, and the texture is spongy and kinky. I like how it feels and how it looks on me, but something about it now feels wrong. "I know what I have to do," I tell myself. "This is old growth hair. It has to go. Symbolically, it represents who I used to be."

On the morning after our horseback descent into the Venado Valley, the trek leaders, Shelly and Nancy, gathered our group together in the barn.

"This is a muscle testing exercise," Shelly explained. She walked Juano the stallion into the open arena space. Trek participants stood to the side.

"Use your mind's eye to scan your entire body," she instructed us. "Then notice the place that is strongest in your awareness. What kind of quality does it have?"

Without question, the most pronounced pain I had was in my neck. Normally I didn't notice it too much, but now that my mind was focused and my eyes were closed, I could feel the stiffness and tension in those muscles. I'd been having neck pain every morning upon awakening for over a year and a half. Chiropractic care had helped a great deal, but the pain had never disappeared entirely.

"Now open your eyes," Shelly instructed us. "Look at Juano while you keep your awareness on that part of your body. What do you feel now?" Each participant was asked to share with the group the sensations that arose as a result. But I was distracted and barely able to pay attention. When my turn came, Juano spoke to me:

> *The pain you have been carrying in your neck will stay with you until you finish grieving the change in your family. It's been with you for a while now, and nothing will relieve it completely except the grieving you still need to do.*

"What are you talking about?" I answered him silently.

My turn to speak to the group had come. Everyone was waiting for me to share. I thought I knew what Juano was talking about.

"It's the loss of my family life and the divorce," I told the group. "I've been trying so hard to be strong, to get on with my life and be courageous for my children."

I'd felt the sorrow and the disappointment, so what was there left to grieve?

I looked at Juano and saw that he was looking back at me. My neck muscles tightened and stung. I took in a deep breath.

"What, Juano? What do I need to do?" I whispered. I could feel the pain intensifying as Juano sent healing energy my way.

Just feel what needs to be felt, and see what needs to be seen. Then you'll be able to grieve.

I thought I'd done that work already. Obviously, it wasn't complete. There were many remaining elements to grieve, including the many in-laws and friends who I'd come to know and love in the context of my marriage. And I had not wanted to acknowledge the guilt I felt over the tremendous pain the divorce had inflicted on my son and daughter, or my failure to stay in my marriage "til death do us part." I'd let down my in-laws, my parents, and my community, and I felt I was no longer the woman I always thought myself to be. Because it was more than I could bear to feel emotionally, the pain got stuck in the back of my neck where every morning, when I woke to a new day that should have been full of bright promise, it would remind me of the punishing, unrelenting judgment I had passed on myself. It was time to grieve the false self I'd created, to forgive myself, and to allow myself to stop trying to live up to an ideal that I could never attain.

That night I asked Juan José for a pair of scissors. An inner transformation was moving inside of me. Part of me was dying, never to return, and part of me was yet to emerge.

Juan José held the scissors in his hand.

"But why is she cutting it off?" Juan José's mother asks him as she and others gather around in shock and curiosity. I explain in the best Spanish I can muster that divine grace has touched me through Conan, and that removing my hair is a symbolic sacrifice. Holy Spirit is asking something of me from a place far beyond my own will and awareness. Inner transformation is erupting, like the volcano, making me fertile ground ready for new growth.

And I am saying, "Yes."

Juan José's mother quietly cries as she watches each person take a turn in cutting the twists of my hair: Juan José, his wife Cendri, their daughter and son, five of my fellow trekkers, our leaders, Debbie, the cook, and the massage therapist all take turns removing my hair until I am left with barely a shadow covering my scalp. I lower my head and close my eyes, opening my heart to the will of God's spirit within me.

Once my hair is off, everyone begins to disband. The trekkers head to their bunkrooms over the barn, and I start to go to the main house on the hill where I am staying with Debbie and the rest of the leadership team. But those three have more to do, more to discuss, to arrange for the next day of the program, so I head up to the house on my own. The hill beyond the barn is steep but the driveway is clear, mostly hard-packed dirt with a short grassy cover. It's about a five-minute walk up, which in daylight is relatively easy. Walking it at night is harder because there is very little illumination. One dimly lit, yellow bulb atop a single electric poll offers the only light on the path, and it is at the very bottom of the driveway. No lights are on at the house, so my destination is shrouded in shadows. And I don't have a flashlight.

Alone under the single light, I contemplate what to do next. Too tired to wait for my fellow team members, I push on into the darkness. I can see nothing, not even my feet or the ground below, in the pitch black of night. Once again, I feel the fear of the unknown, the sense of having no control, of vulnerability and possible danger. Is this an irrational fear? Perhaps. But I can't even see the house, nor tell where the edge of the steep driveway is. I am afraid to walk this path alone.

I turn back towards the barn where my colleagues are talking. I wait a while for them, but they can't see me. After about ten minutes, I summon the courage to try again to go back to the house. But fear rises and slows my gait to a standstill.

Divine Presence, I need your help.

The prayer is barely uttered when I hear the sound of barking. Suddenly, right at my feet is a medium-sized black dog, and right behind him two others, one of whom I recognize as Debbie's little dog, Beanie. She's been with us for the entire trek, keeping up every step of the way.

"Hi there, you guys!" I say. "Have you all come to walk me home?"

Two of them take off into the darkness and head straight for the house. Beanie stays with me, close enough for me to sense her and to feel confident of where I am stepping. Before I know it, I am opening the front door.

"Thank you, Beanie," I say. "Goodnight."

X

A MESSAGE TO HUMANS
FROM BEAUTY

On Beauty's urging, I'd sat alone in my cabin at Leaves and Lizards Arenal Cabin Retreat. I shifted into a state of receptivity as she'd instructed me to do, listening as she spoke. She'd told me to take notes. Here is what was written:

This is a message to humans from Beauty, speaking on behalf of all horses.

We are horses, as you call us. Now, do you want to know who we really are? We've been waiting for you to ask. Please listen with your heart and with your solar plexus. If you try to understand solely with your intellect, you will not understand.

We came to earth when you did. We came as your companions. It did not take very long for you humans, as you call yourselves, to find us and to bring us into your lives. We did not come easily into your care. It took time. This is because we'd forgotten who we were, just as you had. Now, we are beginning to remember, just as you are.

Hear this with your heart.

We are beginning to remember, which means we are no longer as willing to continue the same kind of relationship we have always had with you. We are awakening to our purpose, as you are. This means that we are changing rapidly.

Change with us, and our companionship will continue. Otherwise, you will find that horses all over the world will begin to disagree with the terms you have given us. We want a new relationship with you.

Here is an example from Rosa's own memory. It is one of many thousands:

A woman decides to buy horses, to make horseback riding her hobby. She joins a hunt club. She has wonderful times riding with her friends across the beautiful countryside. A decade goes by, and her life changes. The lovely house, barn, fields, and horses no longer fit who she sees herself to be. She finds a new job, packs up the house, and moves away. The horses are sold. There are three in all. They are each sent to a different new owner.

That may sound reasonable to you. As you begin to change, however, to awaken to who you are, to who we are to you, such a scenario will be horrifying. You will not let this happen.

Many of us are bred to run so that you humans can be entertained, but mostly so that you can enjoy the thrill of immediate monetary gain. Great elaborate schemes are created to orchestrate the fiasco that is our life. When you wake up to the true nature of our purpose together with you on this earth, this will be intolerable and appalling.

Already this gives you pain, and you want to go back to sleep and forget what is revealed. As you begin to open your eyes, your hearts, and your solar plexus to experience us as the beings that we truly are, you will feel pain and discomfort. Each of you will *experience this in your own way. Ask our forgiveness. We will for-give, and then you will feel exhilaration.*

Remember. We came to Earth together and therefore, in many ways, were alike. Our origins in the universe are exactly the same. Our purpose for being here is the same as well.

This leads me to why.

It will be no surprise to you that Earth was formed as one of many places that make learning possible. The momentum, the forces, the energy, and especially the light of the sun are all part of the combined creative energies that foster the growth of conscious-ness. That is our sole purpose in being in this form. We are here for the growth of our consciousness, just as humans are.

There are many humans who once lived as horses, but fewer horses have ever lived as humans. What matters is that we have been living and evolving in consciousness together, in an awareness of the "I Am" that you are familiar with, for millions of years. This is a rebirthing process, which for the human-horse collective has taken thousands of years. We are nearing the end of that pro-cess, which, like physical birth, can be quite painful and dangerous.

"How is it dangerous?" you will ask. Well, consider the pro-cess of leaving one state of being where your consciousness and all your senses are accustomed to one environment, and then suddenly being exposed to an entirely different array of stimuli. The adjust-ment is not always an easy one. Everything changes, from how oxygen is taken in (the breath), to how nourishment is taken up (the stomach), to how the world is felt (the skin), to how the world is seen (the eyes). The old ways of knowing and being will soon no longer work.

We horses and humans are in the process of moving from one way of being and knowing into another. We are doing this together, humans and horses, as we fulfill our purpose on Earth.

XI

AN ANCIENT STORY, RETOLD

When the Horses Whisper is a story I've been led to write. It is an ancient tale, and entirely true. We all have the capacity to hear this truth, even though modern life has caused many of us to forget its core message. It's a story that has been told since we emerged as humans, and it concerns our interconnection with the non-human world—the "natural" world, from which we have become estranged through over-reliance on the cognitive functions of our human cerebral cortex. These faculties, including thinking, perceiving, and understanding language, have served us well in many ways, but they also can cut us off from the rest of ourselves, including our bodies, our deeper wisdom, and our ability to connect with other species.

But if we look at human history, we find it replete with animals, in legend and lore. Beginning with the oldest cave paintings, and continuing into the print and electronic media of current times, animals are deeply embedded in our stories because they inform our ways of understanding the world. Since humanity's beginnings, they have helped us to survive and thrive: not just materially as resources for food, clothing, and labor, but symbolically as well. Through the millennia and across the cultural spectrum, they have appeared as our totems, mystical symbols, and guides, representations of archetypal forms and divine energies. More recently, they show up as our companions, guides, and friends. But who are these creatures, really? More importantly, what are they becoming, and what are they inviting us to become?

Of late, I find myself encountering animals in more and more ways that surprise me and teach me. On a March visit to Ocracoke Island, North Carolina, Bill and I took a walk on the 15-mile National Seashore. As far as the eye could see we were the only people there on this late afternoon. I delighted in the scent of the ocean, the tumbling sea foam, and the running sandpipers and plovers as we strolled on the packed white sand between the grassy dunes and the rolling breakers. Catching sight of a larger bird sitting at the edge of the surf, we moved in its direction. It did not move away as we approached. "What is it doing here?" we wondered. "What is the matter with that bird?" Neither of us was sure what kind of bird it was until it made the distinctive call of the common loon. We spend time by a New Hampshire lake in the summer, and are very fond of these magnificent birds, whose calls fill the night and invite us deeper into our dreams and the mysteries of that realm. It was thus all the more shocking and appalling to witness this pathetic spectacle. We stood helpless, trying to come to terms with what seemed the inevitability of its death; painfully aware of our powerlessness in the face of forces we could not change.

That night, we viewed a streaming documentary, *Dark Side of the Loon*. From it we learned that immature loons are left on their own, heading out from their places of birth on the Northern lakes, only after their parents have first departed for Southern shores. The fledglings make the long flight south, to navigate the challenges of the southern, salt-water environment, remaining there up to three years, largely on their own. Even then, adult loons lose flight plumage each winter, and must exist on what the sea provides. Many die of emaciation if conditions don't go the right way. This winter had been rough, beginning with Super Storm Sandy and continuing through another big storm the week prior to our visit. The heavy wave action and powerful currents can make shore waters murky, with visibility too poor for the loon to hunt. So we deduced that this one was probably emaciated from hunger, and learned that rescue was rarely successful in such cases. But we did not know this while we stood on that beach, helplessly watching the loon turn its head this way and that, wailing now and then; we could only feel our hearts go out to this beautiful creature. I looked up and down the beach for some vessel that we might use to rescue this bird. But there was nothing. We finally accepted the fact that we'd be leaving that bird to finish this struggle on its own.

Even as our hearts were sinking at this realization, we came to see that the loon looked quite calm, even accepting it seemed, without any sense of doom or anguish, without "forethought of grief," as the poet Wendell Berry terms it. The tide was coming in. It wouldn't be long before he'd either be claimed by the rising sea, or find the strength to live on. I felt the turbulence of my inner struggle as I watched him sitting there peacefully. At that moment, he opened his beak and let out a second cry, the high, haunting wail that loons use to find each other. It was weak and whimpering, yet it carried upward on the wind. The sound pierced my heart, opening the place in me where I feel the power of my own longing for that which connects us. "Goodbye and safe journeys," I said to my friend. Bill offered his own blessings, and we walked away.

What did the loon say to me? What did we learn from this encounter? Indeed, I saw the dark side of the loon; its magnificence and plumage stripped away, as just another fellow being trying to survive in a risky world. I felt jolted back into mindfulness of my own vulnerability and lack of control in my own life. Back on the lake in New Hampshire, lulled to sleep by its melodic sound, we had built a nice, comforting image of the loon as a mysterious creature whose beautiful music filled the night. We had perhaps assumed that the loons fled their Northern lakes as the ice set in, spending a winter life of ease on warm Southern shores. We had not known the full story of the loon's life: its flightless helplessness on winter oceans, or its solitary young life, spending up to three years away before returning to the breeding grounds. As this fuller picture was laid out before me, I felt gifted with an insight that helped me understand this creature, and helped me feel our connection in a new way. In its own way, this encounter accorded me a lesson similar to those I have received from being with horses.

While Earth and her creatures appear to be increasingly influenced by human will, what I have learned from listening to horses suggests that the extent of our influence may have been overestimated. Some scientists have dubbed these current times as the "Anthropocene" epoch, on the grounds that current and future conditions on Earth are increasingly determined by human activities. While there is certainly evidence in the sphere of environmental impacts such as climate change that humans are dramatically reshaping our physical world, on deeper levels there are forces at work that humans are only dimly aware of. My experience with horses suggests that if we want to solve the massive challenges we see manifesting in the physical realm as environmental damage, we must heal that of ourselves we which experience as fearful, retracted or empty, reaching into the deeper emotional and spiritual realms to find the missing pieces we need. Only then might we bring ourselves into balance and make our world whole again.

For the first many millennia of human existence, we lived in a physical, mental, and spiritual world in which we belonged to a great and complex web of life, in which all creatures were intertwined. In the last few millennia, humans have come to believe ourselves to have dominion over the earth and its creatures. Whether that belief comes from the Bible or from the ego-awareness associated with our advancing intellects, it has been formative to our consciousness and fundamental to our behavior.

Though we are living longer and healthier lives than ever before, many still strive in vain to glean the meaning and purpose of life. We are also beginning to realize that our current understandings and behaviors and their impacts on the earth are unsustainable. This growing realization leaves many of us questioning our habitual roles on this planet, and wondering whether and how to redefine those roles. Could it be that we have lost our way? That's what my experience leads me to believe. What I see is that we are in the process of rediscovering ourselves, physically, emotionally, and psychologically. These discoveries stem from evolutionary adaptation, but also from technological changes we have made to alter our bodies and our environment. We are learning to shift our perceptions about who we are, why we are here on the earth as human beings, and what it means to be fully alive.

As we humans continue to evolve our sense of being, our notion of what—and who—animals are is also evolving. We are re-awakening to the understanding of humans belonging to the earth—not vice versa—and of humans being part of the life force that sustains it, along with the other species we share it with. *Soul-of-horse* offers us its loving assistance. And if we listen, and learn to trust it, we might actually hear a still, small voice that is leading us back home.

Unknown Costa Rican horse

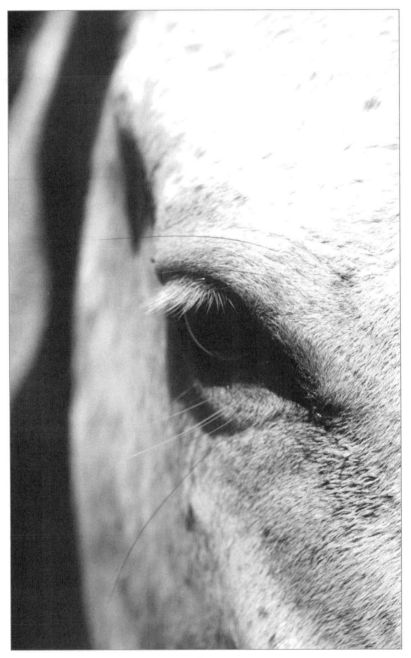

Suzy

Blue Star and Stevie

ABOUT THE AUTHOR

Photo by Nina Fuller

Rosalyn W. Berne, Ph.D. explores the intersecting realms between emerging technologies, science, fiction, and myth, and between the human and non-human worlds. As a university professor she writes and teaches about engineering and technology in society and the ethical implications of technological development, often using science fiction material in her classes. In her personal life she continues to discover the transformational nature of human-equine relationships, and offers facilitation and translation services for enhancing communication between horses and their owners. She is author of *Nanotalk: Conversations with Scientists and Engineers About Ethics, Meaning, and Belief in the Development of Nanotechnology* (Earlbaum Press, 2005) and the novel *Waiting in the Silence* (Spore Press, 2012). The sequel to that novel, *Walking on the Sea*, is currently underway. *To Recreate Life from Life: Biotechnology and Science Fiction* brings the non-fictional writing of research scientists together with Berne's science fiction short stories (forthcoming from Pan Stanford Press). *When the Horses Whisper,* her first foray into the human–animal sphere of interconnection, delves into the inner world of horses, and her own.

ABOUT THE PHOTOGRAPHER

Kaya Berne is a native of Charlottesville, Virginia. She currently attends the University of Virgina, where she is double majoring in neuroscience and studio art. After studying extensively under National Geographic photographers Nick Nichols and David Alan Harvey, she continues to develop her style as a freelance photographer and videographer. She plans on incorporating her skills as a visual artist with research in the neuroscience field.

RELATED TITLES

If you enjoyed *When the Horses Whisper,* you may also enjoy other Rainbow Ridge titles. Read more about them at www. rainbowridgebooks.com.

The Cosmic Internet: Explanations from the Other Side
by Frank DeMarco

Conversations with Jesus: An Intimate Journey
by Alexis Eldridge

Dialogue with the Devil: Enlightenment for the Unwilling
by Yves Patak

The Divine Mother Speaks: The Healing of the Human Heart
by Rashmi Khilnani

Difficult People: A Gateway to Enlightenment
by Lisette Larkins

When Do I See God: Finding the Path to Heaven
by Jeff Ianniello

Dance of the Electric Hummingbird
by Patricia Walker

Coming Full Circle: Ancient Teachings for a Modern World
by Lynn Andrews

Thank Your Wicked Parents
by Richard Bach

The Buddha Speaks: To the Buddha Nature Within
by Rashmi Khilnani

*Consciousness: Bridging the Gap Between Conventional Science and the
New Super Science of Quantum Mechanics*
by Eva Herr

Jesusgate: A History of Concealment Unraveled
by Ernie Bringas

Messiah's Handbook: Reminders for the Advanced Soul
by Richard Bach

Blue Sky, White Clouds
by Eliezer Sobel

Inner Vegas: Creating Miracles, Abundance, and Health
by Joseph Gallenberger, Ph.D.

Your Soul Remembers: Accessing Your Past Lives through Soul Writing
by Joanne DiMaggio

Lessons in Courage: Peruvian Shamanic Wisdom for Everyday Life
by Bonnie Glass-Coffin, Ph.D. and don Oscar Miro-Quesada

Rainbow Ridge Books publishes spiritual, metaphysical, and self-help titles, and is distributed by Square One Publishers in Garden City Park, New York.

To contact authors and editors, peruse our titles, and see submission guidelines, please visit our website at *www.rainbowridgebooks.com*.

For orders and catalogs, please call toll-free:
(877) 900-BOOK.